James H. Potts

Spiritual Life

Its nature, urgency and crowning excellence - Vol. 1

James H. Potts

Spiritual Life
Its nature, urgency and crowning excellence - Vol. 1

ISBN/EAN: 9783337273729

Printed in Europe, USA, Canada, Australia, Japan

Cover: Foto ©Thomas Meinert / pixelio.de

More available books at **www.hansebooks.com**

SPIRITUAL LIFE:

ITS NATURE, URGENCY, AND CROWNING EXCELLENCE.

BY

REV. J. H. POTTS, A.M.,

AUTHOR OF "PASTOR AND PEOPLE," "THE GOLDEN DAWN," ETC.

NEW YORK:
PHILLIPS & HUNT.
CINCINNATI:
CRANSTON & STOWE.
1884.

PREFACE.

NOT as containing any thing especially new or sensational on the subject of the higher life are the following pages given to the public. Presenting little of the doctrinal or speculative, and nothing of the controversial or dogmatic, they seek only to call attention to the existing necessity for a purer life and a better work in the Churches. The author recently received from a pastor a private letter in which was written : "Unless one is in the direct work of building up souls in Christ, he can hardly be aware of the awful darkness which has settled upon the minds of nine tenths of all Christian people, and the terrible struggle they are making to keep on the 'legal' side of Christian experience."

Perhaps a practical appeal for greater spirituality — an appeal apart from denominational

peculiarities—may meet with more or less acceptance among God's children of every name. Certain it is that something is required to stir up the
pure minds of ministers and laymen every-where
by way of remembrance, both of duty and privilege, in the work of our high calling. That this
unpretentious little book will wholly meet the
demand is too much to expect; that it may serve
some good purpose in this direction is the earnest
hope of   THE AUTHOR.

OFFICE OF
MICHIGAN CHRISTIAN ADVOCATE, }
DETROIT.

CONTENTS.

Blessed be the God and Father of our Lord Jesus Christ, who hath blessed us with all spiritual blessings in heavenly places in Christ: according as he hath chosen us in him before the foundation of the world, that we should be holy and without blame before him in love.—Eph. i, 3, 4.

Create in me a clean heart, O God; and renew a right spirit within me. Cast me not away from thy presence; and take not thy Holy Spirit from me. Restore unto me the joy of thy salvation; and uphold me with thy free Spirit. Then will I teach transgressors thy ways; and sinners shall be converted unto thee.—Psa. li, 10–13.

But whoso looketh into the perfect law of liberty, and continueth therein, he being not a forgetful hearer, but a doer of the work, this man shall be blessed in his deed.—Jas. i, 25.

Be watchful, and strengthen the things which remain, that are ready to die: for I have not found thy works perfect before God.—Rev. iii, 2.

The words that I speak unto you, they are spirit, and they are life.—John vi, 63.

Follow after charity, and desire spiritual gifts. — 1 Cor. xiv, 1.

SPIRITUAL LIFE.

I.

THE LIFE.

SPIRITUAL life! what is it? The expression is very familiar; we have all heard it from childhood up; is the experience equally common? Is it something gained in the order of natural growth, of intellectual development, of social progress, or moral improvement? Is it, in some degree, a heritage of every man's earthly existence, cropping out somewhere and at some time as a necessary part of his being? Or is it a distinct element, introduced by other than natural processes, and requiring in every individual that has it free and intelligent acceptance of it at the hands of the great Giver of all life? Verily, the latter view is correct. Spiritual life is life begotten in the trusting heart by the Spirit of God. The Spirit proceeds from Christ, who is our life. He produces spiritual life in the believer because he

is the very breath of the living and glorified
Christ. He takes of that which belongs to Jesus
(John xvi, 15) and communicates it to us. "Our
Lord's holy life on the earth," says Prof. Godet,
"is the type which the Holy Spirit is commis-
sioned to reproduce in us, the treasury from
which he draws the renewing of our life. Life,
in Scripture, denotes a fully satisfied existence,
in which all the faculties find their full exercise
and their true occupation. Man's spirit, become
the abode and organ of the Divine Spirit, realizes
this life with a growing perfection to eternal
life." In many passages of Scripture Christ is
referred to as dwelling in the believer. This can
be only a spiritual habitation. It is Christ in the
person of the Spirit that joins himself with the
spirit and life of man, they twain constituting a
spiritual life of the highest order known to created existence. Where the Spirit of Christ is
there he is also himself. Christ in us thus becomes our life of joy and our hope of glory. He
satisfies us just in proportion as we awake in his
likeness. He uses us for good in the ratio of our
separation from evil and consecration to his service. "And if Christ be in you, the body is dead
because of sin; but the *Spirit is life* because of
righteousness." Rom. viii, 10. Spiritual life will

not prevent the death of the body, but it will energize the life of the soul, making it potent for good, and in the end will quicken the mortal part, and result in life eternal.

Spiritual life, then, is no "spontaneous generation"—an element springing into being of itself. It is not mere development of latent energies or dormant forces; it is not moral rectitude, nor physical perfection, nor any thing that comes within the range of purely human capabilities. It is a life of God. It is a new creation. It is being born from above, born of the Spirit, made a child of God, and adopted into his family.

And this beginning of spiritual life in man has its striking analogy in nature. It is a wonderful thing, but not more wonderful than the beginning of natural life. Scientists now concede that there is no such thing as life spontaneously generated. Life can only come from pre-existing life. The attempt, such as Bastian hastily made, and supposed successful, to get the living out of the dead has proved a disastrous failure. Huxley is free to grant that the doctrine of life only from life is "victorious along the whole line at the present day." "The present state of knowledge," he says, "furnishes us with no link be-

tween the living and the not living." * Tyndall
affirms that "no shred of trustworthy experimental testimony exists to prove that life in our
day has ever appeared independently of antece-
dent life." †   Life springs only at the touch of
the great Lifegiver. This is nature's law, universal and unchangeable.

And so spiritual life is not the result of merely
good resolves, a reformation of character if it was
previously bad, a gradually becoming better and
better until, from wickedness and degeneracy,
that quality of religious nature known as spiritual life is attained. "Spiritual life," says that
masterly scholar, Professor Henry Drummond, "is
the gift of the Living Spirit. The spiritual man
is no mere development of the natural man. He
is a new creation born from above. As well expect a hay infusion to become gradually more
and more living until, in course of the process, it
reached vitality, as expect a man, by becoming
better and better, to attain the eternal life." He
says again, "The door from the natural to the
spiritual is shut, and no man can open it. This
world of natural men is staked off from the spiritual world by barriers which have never yet been

---

* "Encyclopædia Britannica," (new ed.,) Art., "Biology."
† "Nineteenth Century," 1878, p. 507.

crossed from within. No organic change, no modi-
fication of environment, no mental energy, no moral
effort, no evolution of character, no progress of
civilization can endow any single human soul
with the attribute of spiritual life. The spiritual
world is guarded from the world next in order
beneath it by a law of biogenesis, 'Except a
man be born again, . . . born of water and of
the Spirit, he cannot see the kingdom of God.'
The breath of God, blowing where it listeth,
touches with its mystery of life the dead souls
of men, bears them across the bridgeless gulf between the natural and the spiritual, between the
spiritually inorganic and the spiritually organic,
endows them with its own high qualities, and de-
velops within them these new and secret faculties, by which those who are born again are said
to see the kingdom of God."* This is experience, real, conscious, Christian experience. It is
passing "from death unto life." It is the beginning of a new career, a spiritual existence to
which the soul was before a stranger. The
world calls this change *conversion*, and such it
is. It is a turning from one state to another, a
change, not only of the conduct, but of the heart,
a renewing of the mind, a passing away of the

* "Natural Law in the Spiritual World," p. 71.

old in thought and affection and a coming in of the new, an enthronement within of the holy and good. "If any man be in Christ, he is a new creature: old things are passed away; behold, all things are become new." 2 Cor. v, 17.

In this new life there is growth. While there could not be a growth *into* it, any more than from vegetable life into animal life, there is growth *in* it. The life, once begun, like the life of the body, expands, matures, rises into more and more fullness. The subject of it is earnest, believing, prayerful, self-denying, and a student of the Word, and his growth goes on. He is planted in Christ. He is rooted and built up in him. He abides in the vine, and in the course of events is expected to bring forth fruit. In short, as one says, "the Christian, like the poet, is born, not made; and the fruits of his character are not manufactured things, but living things, things which have grown from the secret germ, the fruits of the living Spirit. They are not the products of this climate, but exotics from a sunnier land." The conditions of growth and fruitfulness are within the compass of every renewed life. As the branch abides in the vine, so the Christian must abide in Christ: he must allow grace, which is as free as the air, as clear as the sunshine, and as refreshing as the dew, to play over him, to bathe his spirit, and invigorate his soul.

If he does this he lives on. Christ lives in him. Christ is his, and he is Christ's. The life of Christ is thus manifest in his mortal flesh. The Spirit of Christ fills him, thrills him, and renders his existence a foretaste of the bliss of heaven.

Of the certainty of the spiritual life, its deep and comforting reality, we are not left without a witness. Paul tells us so. In that wonderfully beautiful chapter, the eighth of Romans, the chapter "beginning with no condemnation, and ending with no separation," he declares, " For as many as are led by the Spirit of God, they are the sons of God. For ye have not received the spirit of bondage again to fear; but ye have received the Spirit of adoption, whereby we cry, Abba, Father. The Spirit itself beareth witness with our spirit, that we are the children of God: and if children, then heirs; heirs of God, and joint heirs with Christ." Here the Spirit is presented as a gracious, loving Guide, a present and powerful Witness, and " the leading " on the one hand, and following on the other, show the fact of sonship in all in whom is the Spirit of

God's dear Son. The word "cry" is emphatic, expressing the spontaneousness and strength of filial recognition. Elsewhere the apostle tells us that the exclamation is drawn from our hearts by the Spirit itself: "And because ye are sons, God hath sent forth the Spirit of his Son into your hearts, crying, Abba, Father." Gal. iv, 6. The cry which proceeds from our own hearts under the vitalizing energy of the Spirit, as the very element of the new life, is responded to by the divine voice setting a distinct seal to ours; and so, "in the mouth of two witnesses," the thing is established. The arms of the believer are stretched out to take hold of God, and at the same time the arms of God are extended to draw to his bosom his child. No sooner does the cry of love, *My Father!* ascend from the seeking heart, than there comes back the comforting response, *My son!* This means adoption, sonship, home, protection, sustenance, inheritance, and heaven. It implies work, worship, prayer, and endurance unto the end. It is the conscious commencement of a spiritual existence, which may unfold in the glories of life eternal.

Commentators are agreed in this. Calvin observes on the above passage, that "if the Holy Ghost did not bear testimony of God's parental love, our tongue would remain silent, for we could not in prayer call him Father, unless we were assured that he really was so." Dr. Whedon understands by the expression, "Spirit itself," the immediate person of the Holy Ghost testifying solely to the fact of our sonship; and by the expression, "beareth witness *with ours,*" that he testifies concurrently with, so that there are two witnesses, the divine and the human, testifying to the one fact that we are the children of God.

Real and true, then, is the work of the Spirit in the soul's salvation. While it is so mysterious and profound that none can comprehend it who have not obtained like precious faith, it nevertheless enters into the consciousness and becomes as much a fact of life as any thing besides. It is an experience which can be clearly perceived and recognized by all who have it. " He that believeth on the Son of God hath the witness in himself." This witness he carries with him. It is a permanent, settled, standing witness which no trial or difficulty, other than the sinful, can dislodge. It is an inward testimony or impression on the soul which unites with the believer's own faculties and powers of understanding, forming a sort of double evidence, which cannot be doubted. The soul as intimately and evidently perceives when it loves, delights, and rejoices in God, as when it loves and delights in the companionship of a friend. The process, like the coming of the light and heat, or the shifting of the wind, is mysterious, but the fact itself is plain enough. To "every one that is born of the Spirit" God hath given an understanding by which he knows him that is true. "The blind man of Scripture," says Rev. Dr. J. B. Aylesworth, "had the witness in himself that he was cured, in the plain, simple, undoubted fact that *he could see.* So he that believeth on the Son of God hath the witness in himself that he is saved. The same as the weeping woman at the Saviour's feet, to whom he said, 'Thy faith hath saved thee, go in peace.' The same as the cleansed leper had, and the woman who had been straightened and loosed from an infirmity of eighteen years' standing. The same as Paul had when he found himself a new creature in Christ Jesus; or as Peter had when he lost his moral cowardice and found himself with holy boldness facing the mob and defending and proclaiming the faith. The same as Fletcher who, after a night spent much in prayer, was greatly encouraged next day because his temper was broken. The same as John Bunyan, who was rebuked for his profanity by a very wicked woman, who told him that he had the name of being 'the most profanest man in the town of Bedford.' He resolved, by the grace of God, never to swear again. And he never did. I also have had similar experience. The habits of youth which I dreaded and feared were my masters, I found easily subdued by the invisible, imperceptible, but none the less mighty and effectual working of the grace of God in answer to prayer,

> 'He breaks the power of canceled sin,
>   And sets the prisoner free.'

And he in whom the power of sin and sinful habits is broken has the witness in himself that God is working in him and saving him just as plainly as had the blind man or the cleansed leper."

Such an experience is worth having. It is the richest, grandest, and most abiding possible to the soul of man. It is the solid ground of that spiritual life which alone is pleasing to God and proof against the insinuations of the evil one.

> " His witness within, by faith we receive,
>   And, ransomed from sin, in righteousness live;
>   Through Jesus's passion we gladly possess
>   A present salvation, a kingdom of peace."

2

II.

THE WORK.

MAN is called to be a worker. He has the best of examples. Jesus said, "My Father worketh hitherto, and I work." Paul was a worker, and he exhorted the Churches that with quietness they work. Every true Christian is a laborer. All are not to be active in the same channel, but none are to be idle. With tongue or pen, hands or feet, wealth or influence, every believer in Christ is bound to be active. An idle Christian is the poorest kind of Christian, if, indeed, he be any Christian at all. How can he gain the things which pertain unto life and godliness? Hear Peter: "Add to your faith virtue; and to virtue, knowledge; and to knowledge, temperance; and to temperance, patience; and to patience, godliness; and to godliness, brotherly kindness; and to brotherly-kindness, charity."

In a sacred book of the East it is said that when a man dies they who survive him ask what property he has left behind. The angel who

bends over the dying man asks what good deeds
he has sent before him. In our better book it is
pronounced,

"Blessed are the dead which die in the Lord. . . .
They may rest from their labors; and their works
do follow them."

In the aggregate we know that Christianity is
doing much, more than skeptics acknowledge,
and more than many people dream. It is easy
to believe the testimony of the five senses, but
not so easy to ground our faith upon the reality
of things spiritual. We can see and hear what
science and art are doing for mankind, but the
kingdom of God is like leaven in the meal, unseen and unheard, yet penetrating and powerful
in its operations. Who can measure the extent
of the hidden religious influences at work in the
minds and hearts of the fifty millions of Ameri-
cans to-day? The thought of God, of immortality, of sin and salvation, of the Bible and of
Christ? Who can tell the good accomplished in
society through the agencies of the Church—her
missionary enterprises, her evangelizing efforts,
and public and social means of grace? Think of
more than eighty thousand Protestant ministers
constantly engaged in direct religious work?
Think of eight or ten millions of members scat-

tered through our communities in country, town,
and city, bearing the Christian name and speaking the language of the spiritual Canaan. Think
of over three hundred and sixty colleges, chiefly
under the management of Christian boards of control, and more than one hundred and thirty theological seminaries, whose specific work it is to train
the minds of the rising generation not only to think,
but to think rightly ; not only to reason, but to
reason in harmony with the higher laws and life
which God has implanted in the human breast.
Think of over three hundred religious newspapers
and periodicals scattering abroad their weekly and
monthly issues like the leaves of autumn. Think
of the various philanthropic and reformatory
agencies which owe their origin and support to
the humane spirit of the age, in turn begotten
and fostered by the living principles and power
of Christianity. Think especially of the tens of
thousands of Sunday-schools every-where at work,
growing more numerous and mighty every week,
and destined to become the grandest agency
known to mankind, for the Christian culture and
training of those who are to occupy positions of
trust and responsibility when the present generation has fallen.

Dr. Daniel Dorchester, in his "Problem of

Religious Progress," makes the following summary:

" 1. That Protestant Christian governments are rapidly and surely obtaining political control of the world.

" 2. That Christianity is increasing in the number of its communicants much more rapidly than the world is growing in population.

" 3. That the recent breaking down of many ancient barriers to Christian progress gives promise to a still greater ratio of increase.

" 4. That Protestantism has not deteriorated in the qualities necessary to an aggressive religious force.

" 5. That Romanism is doomed, though its death may be slow.

" 6. That the United States can never become a Roman Catholic nation.

" 7. That the infidelity of to-day is less potent and successful than that of the last century.

" 8. That the so-called 'liberal' Churches of America utterly fail to keep pace with the growth of population.

" 9. That the 'orthodox' Churches of the United States have, during this century, increased in a greater ratio than the population, and that this ratio is steadily increasing. In

1800 the evangelical Churches had one communi-
cant in 14.50 of the population; in 1850, one in
6.57; in 1870, one in 5.78; in 1880, one in 5.

" 10. That the faith, morals, and spirituality
of the present time will not suffer in comparison
with the past.

" 11. That the higher education of our American youth is chiefly in the hands of the evangelical Churches.

" 12. That the Protestant Christian missions
have been a conspicuous success."

Our high type of morality is the result of
practical religion. Had moralists no standard
save the lives of those who are worse than they
are, how soon would their boasted virtues and
good works dwindle into insignificance and ob-
livion. The exalted precepts of Christ, inwoven
in the whole texture of our intellectual natures,
ringing in the memory from early childhood, and
finding their true element—their responsive life
—in the promptings of every educated conscience,
are a power for good which man cannot measure
by any mechanical rules. Every Church edifice,
with spire pointing toward the city of God, is a
helpful reminder that here we must labor if there
we would rest.

But all these results are only the beginning of

what is to be done. The agencies now employed
are but as a drop that precedes the shower when
compared with those that will be necessary ere
God can rain general righteousness upon this
wicked world.

Consider for a moment the present awful condition of mankind. Go into any rural district
where order, quietness, and morality are supposed to abound. See how God's Sabbaths are
violated, his name profaned, his commandments
broken. See how little there is of true philan-
thropy, righteous zeal, or systematic beneficence,
even among the professedly good. Those who
own the broad acres of this American continent
are doing next to nothing to arrest the spread of
evil and convert the world.

In our great cities there is wickedness enough
to appall the strongest and bravest heart. The
Bishop of Manchester, on a Sunday afternoon in
June, was walking back from the East End of
London, and in his sermon preached that evening
in Westminster Abbey, he told what his eyes
beheld:

"I walked along the Commercial Road, and
through the thronged thoroughfares of White-
chapel and Aldgate. I saw humanity there in
many forms, few of them lovely. There was the

street trader driving his profitable trade; there were the hundreds roaming to and fro without an apparent object, who had no Sunday clothes; there was the shameless harlot, and those who made that woman shameless; and there was the deadly spirit vault, with its bar crowded with young and old men and women asking for poison, from end to end. My wife was with me, and she turned to me and said, 'Well, this is sadder than any thing we have seen in Manchester;' and I thought, Can science or philosophy ever heal these things? Nay, my thought was even sadder than that, for I said to myself, We have let this evil grow and gain such dimensions as that. Can even Christianity, such as we know it, and such as we have allowed it to become—can even Christianity heal it? Could Sodom, could Egypt, could the city in which our Lord was crucified have ever shown sadder, more desperate scenes than these?"

What the Bishop of Manchester saw in London on that bright summer day any minister in our American cities may behold for himself.

So commonplace are the evils of intemperance and harlotry that they are taken for granted, considered rather necessary, and scarcely wished otherwise by many who claim to have the good

of humanity at heart. The same sentiment holds
respecting nearly every species of evil. Apart
from periodical uprisings against certain forms
of vice, the wicked are having their day. Like
those of old, they are committing two evils
against God: they are forsaking God, the fountain of living water, and hewing out to themselves cisterns, broken cisterns, that can hold no
water. The world may be wiser, and popular
morality more wide-spread, than fifty years ago,
but the wisdom is not that which the good old
Bible commends, nor is the morality of that
higher Christian type which gives proof of purity
within. There have been social developments
within the last decade startling in the extreme.
They have not yet ceased or diminished. Society
is constantly on the very tiptoe of expectation.
What next? is the anxious inquiry of every good
heart.

Increasing laxity of opinion in respect to the
sanctity of the marriage relation is an alarm-
ing fact. The ratio of divorce to marriage in
some of the States is already one to ten, and
seems to be increasing. To the one ground of
divorce which Christ's precepts allow, human legislators have added a dozen—cruelty, drunken-
ness, contagious or incurable disease, insanity, and

even incompatibility of temper being among the number. In one of the United States, according to President Theodore D. Woolsey, the judges are left absolutely free to grant divorce when they think that the happiness of the marriage relation requires it. Keep on, and the time is not far distant when the marriage service, to be consistent, must read, "as long as we agree," instead of "until death us do part."

It will not do. Christians must bestir themselves, throwing their voices and influence against any laws granting dissolution of the marriage bond for reasons not justified by the teachings of Christ and of Paul. Society will suffer, and the Church be injured more and more, unless this tide of loose sentiment is turned. Without some religious sense of the nature and ends of marriage the sanctity of the marriage relation, in the face of license and lust, cannot be sustained. For this needed religious feeling the Church and ministry are almost solely responsible. Ministers must preach it, laymen must talk it. In Christ's stead they must plead for the integrity and sacredness of the marriage bond and the purity and welfare of the home. In no other instance did our blessed Lord alter or amend the law of Moses, and his direct and clear command in this single case ought to be respected by the Christian world until the present dispensation closes, and time shall be no more. In all cases of Church discipline for divorce, and other offenses against marriage, the authorities should seek to realize in law and justice a true conception of the Saviour's legislation. "If the Christian legislator," says an able authority, "does not carry out Christ's principles in regard to divorce, it will be not because they are moral rather than jural, but because the hardness of men's hearts prevents the introduction of a perfect rule."

Consider the popularity of the play-house. It is an age of lightness and amusement. The theaters in the City of New York alone receive more money than all the Churches in America are contributing for the support of missions. In all other cities theaters have been sustained in a way most flattering to the proprietors and actors, but uncomplimentary to the influence of ministers and Churches.

None can deny that the patronage of the theater is of questionable propriety. There never was a time when pure Christianity did not revolt from the practical influences of the stage. Ministers in all ages have denounced it, moralists have reasoned against it, and those who have defended it have done so on the score of the intellectual rather than the moral.

Even the more virtuous pagans condemned this amusement as injurious to morals and the interests of nations. Plato, Livy, Xenophon, Cicero, Solon, Cato, Seneca, Tacitus, the most venerable men of antiquity, have denounced it as a source of pollution, assuring us that both Greece and Rome had their ruin accelerated by a fatal passion for these corrupting entertainments.

Lord Macaulay affirmed, "The theater is the seminary of vice." Macready, England's star actor, declared, "None of my children, with my consent, under any pretense, shall enter the theater, nor associate with play actors or actresses." An English writer, in the time of Charles I., made a catalogue of authorities against the stage, which contains almost every name of eminence in the heathen and Christian world.

The American Congress, soon after the Declaration of Independence, passed a resolution condemning the stage, and classing it with horse-racing, gaming, etc.

M. Dumas, who wrote "Camille," once said, "You do not take your daughter to see my play. You are right. Let me say, once for all, you must not take your daughter to the theater. It is not merely the work that is immoral, it is the place. Whenever we paint men, there must be a grossness that cannot be placed before all eyes; and whenever the theater is elevated and loyal, it can live only by using the color of truth. The theater being the picture or satire of the passions and social manners, it must be immoral—the passions and social manners themselves being immoral." Edwin Booth, in a letter to the "Christian Union," says, "I never permit my wife or daughter to witness a play without previously ascertaining its character. . . . While the theater is permitted to be a mere shop for gain, open to every huckster of immoral gimcracks, there is no other way to discriminate between the pure and base than through the experience of others."

The secular press of to-day, while upholding the play-house, often confesses to its demoralizing character. The Chicago "Times" says, "Trash of the most unadulterated description has largely taken possession of the stage." Another Chicago paper says, "Twenty-five years ago, such an exhibition as is nowadays nightly made in this class of amusements (modern comic opera) in the most matter-of-fact way, would have gone nigh to landing the whole party in the police station."

The "Detroit Free Press," of February 19, 1882, spoke of one theatrical combination appearing in Detroit, "where sundry gods did seem to set their seals to give the (local) world assurance that there is occasional escape from the reign of rot."

Mark you, only "occasional escape" from general rottenness.

Mr. J. H. M'Vicker, proprietor of a Chicago theater, grants that there is a bad side to the theater, but, of course, considers it unfair to rank his own high-toned house with what he himself terms "shows that are not fit for a decent man or a pure woman to see." But the trouble is, the vile shows form the bulk of the plays, and they must all be sustained in order to get out of the whole mass a minimum of decency.

The trend of the stage is downward, and has always been so. Moral degeneracy is its characteristic. Whoever it catches in its train goes downward with it, or is saved so as by fire. Where it teaches one virtue it hints upon a dozen vices, or possibly parades them openly. Shakespeare himself, the prince of dramatists, whose characters live forever in a pure home, is best read in an expurgated edition of his works. If this is true of Shakespeare, what shall be said of the body of sensational stuff which chiefly crowds the bulletin boards, and appeals to the baser instincts of man's already corrupted nature? The New York "Evening Post" styles it "the feverish slop of a French melodrama," etc.

It is not necessary to attend the theater to gain wisdom to "denounce what is bad in it." The only qualification needed is to look at the show-bills, and then inquire of some bloated attendant whether the female actors "filled the bill."

Dr. Talmage charges upon the average American theater much of the unhealth of this country. "The man who sits night after night until ten or eleven o'clock in the theater, and then takes his oysters and his ale, and crawls into his bed at twelve or one o'clock, will be a sick man. No physical constitution can endure it. The nerves shattered, the imagination excited, the strength exhausted, he will be eaten up by disease, and pitch into an early grave. The American theater has filled the land with a army of invalids. We see them dying with dyspepsia, with neuralgia, with liver complaints, with consumptions, and there is congratulation in hell that the theater killed them. It is death to a man to be busy all day in a store, the air poisoned and corrupt, and then, as a usual thing, to spend three hours at night in a theater, the atmosphere of which is made up ten parts of cologne, fifty parts of tobacco, one part of oxygen, and three hundred and seventy parts of poor whisky. O I have seen the average American theater throw upon society a great many weak, inane, and corrupt men, unfit either for living or dying. I knew a man in this city who was once foremost in the Church, who came under the fascinations of the American theater. He gave up the Sabbath. He gave up the Bible. He gave up God. He came to deny even his own existence, adopting the absurd theory that every thing is imaginary. He went thirty nights in succession to see Macbeth in the old Broadway Theater. It blasted him body and soul."

The theater is the foe of domestic weal. Parents commit their tender babes to the mercy of hired help while they are off satiating a depraved taste for sensation and display.

The theatrical profession is characterized by corruption and cruelty. This is the rule, and for any exception to it we will be as quick to rejoice as any one besides.

It is told that a Church member went behind the curtains of a theater and there witnessed a scene more tragic than any of the fictitious ever performed upon the stage. One of the actors early in the evening received a summons to the bedside of his dying sister, but was not permitted to leave until the play was finished and death had come.

"The sister of a female actor," says the "Northern Christian Advocate," "recently fell from a bridge behind the curtains, a distance of thirty feet, and was taken up dying. Did the play cease? Were the audience informed of the accident and requested to bow their heads during the mysterious and solemn process of a soul passing into eternity? No; it was considered of paramount importance that those people should have the full measure of what they paid their money for. By acting thus did not that manager appraise a soul? Alas! how cheap."

But Christians attend the theater. God help them!

There is an old fable which represents that in a certain city Satan observed a Christian at a theater, and at once seized him. As he was about to depart with him some one shouted, "That man is a Christian!" But Satan answered, "The territory of all theaters is mine, and whoever I find thereon I claim."

Proprietors of theaters claim the sympathies

3

of all people found on their territory. Occasionally they make up an exceptionally good programme, advertising that no act or word or scene will be tolerated that can offend the purest mind, and all the Christians they thus draw to the one high-toned performance they quote and parade as the friends and supporters of the theater as it is, "the house whose common and most characteristic features are an offense to purity, to religion, and to God." Thus every reputable patron of the theater, albeit he himself cannot be pointed at as on the high road to destruction, unwittingly becomes an influential, because quoted, supporter of an institution which is sending its multitudes every year farther and farther in the way to hell.

The cry made by the friends of the theater that Christian ministers and laymen ought to give the theater their countenance, and thus reform it, instead of giving it over to the devil and his allies, is the veriest bosh. Were the theater worth reforming, its case is utterly hopeless. A reformed theater is not a theater. There is no reform for the institution. History shows that whenever reformation has been attempted, it has ended in signal defeat. Hannah More withdrew from the stage, and renounced her dramatic productions, because she despaired of the reformation of the stage, and regarded it in its present state as "unbecoming the appearance or countenance of a Christian."

The time is coming when all who esteem virtue worth defending and morality worth maintaining will have to lift up their voices against the bald indecency and profanity of the average modern stage.

All theater-goers inhale for the time being an atmosphere infected with the contagion of irreligion, and it is doubtful whether all entirely recover from the effects. You cannot be present in a room filled with tobacco smoke without carrying away a taint of it; no more can you stay in the presence of morally infected air without bearing away with you the memory of a sneer or slur that will permanently injure your soul.

The attendance of Christians upon the theater is disastrous in its influence upon others, especially the young, who are not professors of religion. Let the members of any Church go to the theater, even once each in five years, but scattering along so that some one represents the Church every few weeks, and sinners, who are always present, naturally conclude that the stage is patronized and supported by the Church.

Church authorities, with few exceptions, condemn theater-going, and have standing rules against it. Every member of the Methodist Episcopal Church who attends the play-house, and will not heed private reproof against it, is liable to arrest of character for imprudent conduct. (See Discipline, 1880, ¶ 226.) Other Churches look with similar disapproval upon theater-going. The Presbyterian ministers of Chicago, at a recent meeting, resolved that "the General Assemblies of 1818 and 1865 justly pronounced" the theater "a school of immorality," and that "the theater, as managed in Chicago, is an open gate-way of perdition, and in effect, if not in intention, is a persistently dangerous attack on the sacredness of family life."

Let the theater be abolished. To this end all Christians should bring themselves into sympathy with Rev. Dr. Herrick Johnson's programme:

"1. The theatrical management held up to public scorn and social ostracism, that deliberately arranges, by purchase or hire, for the shameful exhibition of 'women and girls,' or the representation of plays where heroines are courtesans gilding a shameless career with sensuous fascination. 2. A season of State-prison made sure to the man or men guilty of the exhibition of licentious plays, just as it is provided now for the sale of licentious literature. 3. An aroused and sensitive public sentiment that would make patronage of an immoral play-house disreputable. 4. A conscience that would make every wearer of Christ's name willing to lose his right hand rather than that hand should open the door to the theater, and so give to its moral abominations, even by appearance, the sanction of Christian profession. 5. Meanwhile an earnest, persistent, loving, aggressive preaching, by speech and life, of that sweet and mighty Gospel, the touch of whose very garments has so often made pollution blossom into purity, to which we owe all we have of purity to-day in our hearts and homes, and the prevalence of which at last shall glorify all baseness and banish all filth."

What is true of the theater is true, in a measure, of the modern dance. Devout people have no business there. Really pious minds have no pleasure in it. Its tendency is downward, not upward. True Christians of every age have perceived this, and kept themselves aloof from it.

" The martyrs were not votaries of mixed dances. The illustrious names in Christian history are not names of dancers who danced for amusement. The men who, in the name of God,

came to the rescue of the world in the Dark Ages,
and, by the brightness of their rising, scattered
the night of mankind, did not go to their master-
ful work 'tripping the light fantastic toe.'

"The most of them declaimed against it;
Church councils, again and again, have spoken
against it; even the heathen virtue of Rome in
the days of Cicero led him to say, ' *Nemo fere sal-
tat sobriui nisi forte insanit* '—'No man dances
when he is sober unless he is insane.' William
Carvosso and John Fletcher, men whose characters were almost seraphic, did not dance. John
Wesley did not waltz through his mission of
evangelism. The great lights of Christian history have not gleamed in ball-rooms.

" You cannot begin a dance with prayer. Men
have asked blessings at tables on which were
wine and strong drink; men who kept slaves, and
bought and sold their fellow-creatures like cattle,
have yet had family altars, and in some cases even
prayed for those they traded in; hypocrites have
tortured religion into every shape that would serve
them, and travestied it on every occasion when it
could canse merriment: few things which claim
respectability have failed to be sanctified by
prayer, soon or later; but I have yet to hear of
the first public ball or private hop which com-

menced with supplication or closed with benediction.

"If you could conceive it possible that a person
could begin an evening's dance in a prayerful
mood, you cannot conceive it possible that he
should continue it in that mood. You would as
soon expect a soul to find the Lord in a theater,
or that a wanderer would be reclaimed in a bill-
iard room, as that any dance should begin or end
with a formal, sincere, humble recognition of
God.

"The people who most feel the need of God
and pray most are not there, and thus as a rule
there is nobody to pray.

"Then the thing itself is not a prayerful thing
—it has no aspiration as high as heaven; its spirit
is vain and frivolous; its essence, display; its end,
ephemeral sensuous pleasure or applause: it is
'of the earth, earthy.'"*

Alas! for those of the Christian name who sustain the dance. It is proof quite sufficient that
for them religion is no satisfying portion. Where
Christ fully satisfies there is little going out of
the way in search for pleasure and joy. The
world of fashion and frivolity has few allure-
ments for minds that bear the image of the heav-

* Rev. J. H. Bayliss, D.D.

enly. Let dancing Christians consider whether they have ever known Christ.

Nor is open wickedness the only trouble. Growing indifference to religious services is a matter of remark throughout all the cities of the United States. It is noted also in England. Rev. Newman Hall says that there is throughout that country a diminishing attendance on public worship. As a rule, he adds, that in the large English towns skilled artisans ignore ecclesiastical arrangements. He does not pretend to say that they are aggressively hostile or intensely infidel, but that they are indifferent to ordinary public services; that, as a class, they do not go to Church; that, also, to a large extent, this is true among the upper ranks of fashion, wealth, and intellect. He regrets, too, that a majority of English church-goers content themselves with the morning service on Sunday, leaving the churches almost empty in the evening. He figures it that London has four millions of people, of whom one half might at one time be at church; but for these two millions there is only accommodation for one half, and of these one million of seats only five hundred thousand are at any time occupied.

It is doubtful whether New York, Philadelphia,

Chicago, or Boston can make a better showing. Certain it is that for every church-goer in our land there ought to be five, and for every active member there should be a dozen. The state of religion in any country is a true index of its entire condition—moral, civil, and political. Consequently such facts and figures are by no means reassuring to the religious, the patriotic, or even to the man of the world. Practical piety is the bulwark of national safety. "Whoever does any thing," says Macaulay, "to depreciate Christianity is guilty of high treason against the civilization of mankind."

Nor will truth permit the Churches themselves to be ignored in this inquiry. There is hardness of heart in many that bear the Christian name. If they feel any concern for the danger of the ungodly, they do not show it. If they have any confidence in God, they do not manifest it. If they are moved and guided by the Spirit of truth and love, they give no indication of the same by sweet and heavenly tempers and earnest, hearty service.

Look at the worldly spirit in the Church! Consider the eager pursuit of pleasure and riches and honor. How much more time is spent and more interest felt in obtaining property and ease and enjoyment than in seeking the kingdom of God! How much more talk about the price of land, grain, stock, merchandise, produce, and the various means of getting rich, than about the conversion of sinners and the progress of holiness. How frequently, too, Christians get warmly and deeply engaged about unimportant matters — some party strife, or social question, or financial plan—when the state of their own hearts and the condition of those around them ought to be the chief concern.

A view of the danger of sinners ought to fill Christians with concern. If these persons were in a burning building where escape depended upon the exertions of their fellows, what efforts would be instinctively put forth for their deliverance. But a greater motive to move in their behalf is the fact that they are dishonoring God by their wickedness, and are momentarily exposed to helpless perdition. When one thinks of these things, it seems almost strange that Christians every-where are not running the streets warning their fellow-men, and at intervals beseeching God to arise and plead his own cause. The salvation of the wicked is far from being hopeless, and, moreover, the radical conversion of a wicked man is worth unbounded labor. The satisfaction which such a case gives to the toil-worn worker repays a thousand-fold.

It is a sad commentary on the state of our religious lives that all these things exist, and we apparently feel very little interest in them or grief about them. Unnumbered evils can be removed when the Church is thoroughly alive to their removal. But when Christians themselves are dead, or nearly so, having little or no faith, prayerless, disobedient, regarding not that sinners are hardening themselves against the truth and perishing in iniquity, then, indeed, is the case desperate, and well may ministers tremble. Never was there greater need than now for the sons of God to "stand upon their watch, and sit upon the watch-tower, to see what the Lord will say unto them, and what they shall answer when they are reproved." Never more need to join with the old prophet and pray, "O Lord, revive thy work in the midst of the years, in the midst of the years make known, in wrath remember mercy."

It is not pleasant to dwell upon this theme. It is more congenial to say, "All is well!" and "Peace! peace!" when in fact nothing is well, and the peace is only the apathy of coldness. There never was a spark of pessimism in our

nature, but we cannot shut our eyes to truth.
The Rev. Dr. Howard Crosby is correct in his
assertion that the Church of God is to-day court-
ing the world. Its members are trying to bring
it down to the level of the ungodly. The ball,
the theater, nude and lewd art, social luxuries,
with all their loose moralities, are making inroads
into the sacred inclosures of the Church, and as a
satisfaction for all this worldliness Christians are
making a great deal of Lent and Easter and Good
Friday, and church ornamentation. It is the old
trick of Satan. The Jewish Church struck on
that rock, the Romish Church was wrecked on
the same, and the Protestant Church is fast
reaching the same doom.

Granted that pretty much all the old forms are
retained in the Churches, and that some of them
are yet popular. This is one chief difficulty.
The forms are lifeless, and save as mementoes of
what has been, are comparatively useless. There
is abundance of organization for aggressive work
and grand achievement. Ministers are better
educated than ever before. They enjoy the confidence of the public. They have fine churches
to preach in, and many intelligent auditors to
listen. Ministers and people are at the fullest
liberty to devise means of usefulness, and open

up new lines of access to the masses of the un-godly. If one half as much practical talent and skill were exercised in behalf of the Church as there is in behalf of business interests and polit-ical concerns, the courts of Zion would be thronged and the theme of religion on every tongue.

It is time for pulpit and pew to be aroused. Let stern truth ring out against lying, fraud, adultery, infanticide, and general worldliness. Let a halt be called in the liberalizing tendency of modern thought. Enough already of the no-hell, hail-brother, all-is-merry creed. It is work-ing disaster. Give us reformers. Give us stanch men of old-time zeal, clothed with modern facili-ties for revolutionizing the popular drift of things. Give us a Martin Luther in Brooklyn, a John Knox in Chicago, and ten thousand Wesleys and Whitefields scattered among the cities and plains, all linked together in a grand brotherhood to slay the man of sin and purge society of its corrupt-ing fountain-heads. Who shall the reformers be? Where are the giants for these days? Never better occasion or a wider field.

What is to be done? In the olden days, when opposition to the aggressive movements of the Church was pronounced and active, Christ's fol-lowers girded themselves for the war, and en-

gaged in the required service with resolute purpose to move forward to victory at any cost.
To-day there is too much half-hearted and uncertain avowal of religious profession, and on the
part of many too little disposition to sacrifice ease
or wealth to further the interests of the Lord's
cause.

It is also to be feared that many are losing
confidence in God. It is a time of rank and out-
spoken skepticism. Even those whose religious
experience ought to make them proof against the
assaults of unbelief have caught the deadly infec-
tion, and are apathetic and cold. It does not
require open wickedness to destroy our confidence in God or God's confidence in us. In-
gratitude, born of neglect of duty; unbelief,
growing out of spiritual coldness: these things
effectually hinder communion with God and drive
the Holy Spirit from us. The apostle styles unbelief the easily besetting sin, and so it is. Without faith—an active, vigorous, appropriating faith
—it is impossible to please God.

Now is the time for action. Now is the time
to contend earnestly together for the faith once
delivered to the saints. It is a critical hour.
God and the Church are challenged to a contest
with Satan and his allies for the ruling spirit in

this republic and in the world. Our strength lies not in argument, nor carnal war, but in religious success, in spiritual achievement. There is a power in converted hearts and holy lives which dumbfounds the adversary and puts him to flight. The shouts of redeemed souls unnerve infidels and silence hell itself. When an unbeliever sees his community stirred throughout, under the preaching and praying of men for whom he has cherished little or no regard, he feels in his heart of hearts that the work is not of man, but of God. Especially is this true when his own neighbors come under the influence and are saved, and when, in spite of all his efforts, he cannot keep the subject of religion out of his own mind for a single hour. More infidels have been converted under direct religious influences than by all the sermons preached, lectures delivered, or books written on the subject of infidelity. These are the works of men, but spiritual awakenings are the power of God.

It is in this kind of religious labor, too, that Christians receive their very best spiritual training. If ever an intelligent man seeks wisdom, it is when he approaches his neighbor to speak an appropriate religious word. If ever a man is drawn out in sympathy, it is when his fellow implores of him counsel and help to relieve his spiritual distress. If ever a man rejoices with joy exceeding, even with a foretaste of heaven's rapture, it is when he sees a religious mourner translated, with streaming eyes and a bounding heart, into the kingdom of God's dear Son. In the Church and in the world, at home and abroad, there is work for the Christian to do. It is his mission on earth. Saved by faith, he will be judged by works. His Bible is full of exhortations to holy labor. Mark the words of Paul, who insisted so strenuously on salvation by faith only:

"Finally, brethren, whatsoever things are true, whatsoever things are honest, whatsoever things are just, whatsoever things are pure, whatsoever things are lovely, whatsoever things are of good report; if there be any virtue, and if there be any praise, think on these things."

III.

IN WEAKNESS.

ARE faith, love, and devotion increasing, or are they declining? A similar question was asked more than eighteen hundred years ago: "When the Son of Man cometh, shall he find faith on the earth?"

Sin has abounded in all ages, and the good people of every generation have nearly despaired of realizing the Christian's blessed hope. There has been much to discourage, much to oppose. Only because God's grace abounds more than sin can his people hold on their way.

> "The only star that never sets,
>   Though all its sister fires may fly—
> The only flower that never droops,
>   Though all its fair companions die—
>   Is fadeless hope."

A more practical question would be, Have I living faith in my own heart? Is my love to God stronger than in other days? Am I more devoted and spiritual than ever before? Am I in all respects ready for the coming of the Son of man?

4

Jesus answered the question put to him by
speaking the parable of the Pharisee and pub-
lican, designing it especially for those "which
trusted in themselves that they were righteous."
That parable is peculiarly applicable at the present time. Self-righteousness now fairly reigns.
The average man thanks God that he is not as
other men are, especially such as exhibit the
spirit of humility, and walk in all the commandments of the Lord blameless. It is a great age
for boasting, not so much of fasting "twice in
the week," as of feasting seven times; not so
much of giving tithes of entire possessions, as of
multiplying possessions and entirely withholding
tithes. There are too many who stand, as did
the Pharisee, and parade their good qualities;
too few who really humble themselves and cry
to God for mercy. It is the weakness and defect
of all our worship and work that we trust God
too little and ourselves too much.

We sometimes think and talk about the millennium, but few have any definite idea of what is
to constitute its peculiar blessedness. They appear to imagine that a great miracle will be
wrought to usher in that glorious day, and that
by some external process or influence all hearts
are to be thrilled with new joy, all eyes filled

with wonderful visions, and all people clothed with visible garments of righteousness. Not so. Though, as Pope sings,

"All crimes shall cease, and ancient frauds shall fail;
Returning Justice lift aloft her scale;
Peace o'er the world her olive wand extend,
And white-robed Innocence from heaven descend;"

yet no miraculous exertion of divine power need be looked for. Rather will the natural religious action of mind on mind, of heart on heart, under the influence of the Holy Ghost, bring about that general reign of peace. The fire of God's love will burn brighter and brighter on every holy altar until the flames of all hearts mingle together, encircling the whole extent of the habitable globe with a common warmth and unbroken illumination.

Why, then, may not the spirit of the millennium be now aroused and enjoyed? Why may not individual Christians have to-day the pure affection and perfect rest of soul which will then be universal? God speaks to-day: "Be ye holy, for I am holy." "Love one another, for love is of God." "My presence shall go with thee, and I will give thee rest." We have the same Bible, the same Saviour, the same Comforter, the same plan of salvation, the same field of action, and the same motives to be pure and spiritual that Christians will have in the time to come. If the universal reign of righteousness is deferred a thousand years, it will be simply because the present and immediately succeeding generation prefer "this poor dying rate" of spiritual life to the fervent love and holy zeal and vigorous work which the people of some future time will show forth, thus realizing the fulfillment of the King's promise: "All the ends of the world shall remember and turn unto the Lord; and all the kindreds of the nation shall worship before thee."

When we contemplate the goodness of God in providing so amply for all our wants, and proffering his own almighty aid to help us in our weakness, we can but say, How short-sighted, foolish, and vain is man, that the race is not already delivered from sin, and the earth blossoming and blooming as the rose! The difficulty is with ourselves. The offense is our own. It is a weakness attaching to perverse human nature. Instead of drawing near to God to receive the blessings he offers us, we go away, refusing to receive his benediction. In our far-off state, our non-receptive attitude, we miss most if not all the precious experiences of the Christian life. Surely for this no one is blamable but ourselves. If we choose to make our home under the shadow of a mountain, observes the " Criterion," " we ought not to complain that the sunlight does not enter there. If we seek a dwelling place in a cavern underground, we ought not to cry out against God for not giving us a blue sky and green fields and flowers and birds. It is all our own doing. The world is wide and full of pleasant places wherein we might fix our abode. If we choose shadows, darkness, and dreariness, shall God be blamed? Do we complain because we have not a larger measure of the Spirit of grace and love in our hearts? Do we sometimes feel that God is afar from us, that the way is dark, and the burdens very heavy? Do we mourn over our coldness and indifference to spiritual things? If this be true, it may be well for us to ask ourselves whether it is not, on the whole, our own fault. Is there nothing standing between us and God? Surely, if we have not a fullness of spiritual gifts, it is not because of the slackness of the Giver, or because of an insufficiency of grace, mercy, and love. If our Christian life is not full of joy and hope, as it should be, it is because we do not open the way for it to flow in upon us from his precious word and from the presence of the Holy Spirit. These gracious influences are all about

us, like the sunlight, and we have only to open
our hearts to let them in. If we do not open to
him who says, 'Behold I stand at the door and
knock,' shall we complain that he does not come
in and sup with us, and we with him? If we
steep our hearts in worldliness, and shut out
from our daily lives all thought of God, need we
wonder that we fall into coldness and indifference?"

Look at the excuses and confessions! Some of
them are honest, and some are mere pretexts.

"O," says one, "when I consider how some
others have lived, and the duties I ought to per-
form, the privileges I ought to improve, and the
indisposition of my own heart, I am led to wonder whether I have any religion at all; whether,
if I have any grace whatever, it is sufficient for
these things."

Says another: "Look at my circumstances and
surroundings; pinched for the necessaries of life,
hard work all the time, ungodly neighbors, and
too indifferent fellow Church members; abstract
piety, which some people preach, cannot exist in
such a state of things."

Says a third: "I have not yet been led down
to that spot where it seemed to me, if all else
were absent, it were enough if Christ were there,

and I was performing his will. It is yet as it has been. Gloomy days will come, worldly cares will huddle together in spite of all efforts to reduce them to an equal pressure; and then come hurry, care, and departure from God, and busy thoughts of other things."

It is natural for the heart, in the midst of its declining zeal, to plead its own cause and find excuses for its own low estate. It is natural, too, to imagine that, amid surroundings more favorable to piety, a higher plane would be reached. This may be true, and yet it is divine power combined with the consecrated energies of a redeemed soul which leads to moral uplifting. The external atmosphere, natural or moral, may have its limited influence, but it is God from whom our help cometh. He is very near every one that calleth upon him, and delayeth not to extend rightfully desired aid. The mere matter of outward circumstances in the work of faith is of trifling consequence. "As thy day, so shall thy strength be," is a promise expressly made for the troubled, the tried, and the unfortunate.

> "Let cares like a wild deluge come,
> Let storms of sorrow fall,"

the soul that has learned to live by practical faith on the Son of God dwells safely and securely, while the individual who knows nothing of this important lesson faints and fails in a place and state most conducive to spirituality.

The greatest drawback, however, in the appropriation of divine help is a want of conviction of its need. Men lose sight of life's great object. Their eyes are blinded that they see not their true mission clearly. Getting money and being happy displace as motives the higher obligations of getting wisdom and being holy. It follows that, with worldly motives, human strength is found more nearly adequate to the accomplishment of life's purposes and plans. The simple conditions of wealth are industry, perseverance, and economy. These, with ordinary business sagacity, are sure to result in a competency in the space of a life-time. Little divine help is needed, sought, or wanted by an American especially, whose mind is set on a fortune. Wealth is the goal for which the millions of this generation are striving. It is one long, general, commanding struggle for financial supremacy that every day stirs society from center to circumference. Not bread to eat simply, or raiment to put on, but money to spend in luxury and extravagance. The interminable conflict between capital and labor rages around this central truth. Great for-

tunes are grouped together in forms of corporations and monopolies to utilize labor at a minimum rate of compensation, for the one primary
purpose of adding to the original capital thirty,
sixty, or a hundred-fold. Now, in all these un-
dertakings, God is left out. "Corporations have
no souls." The good old idea that the judgment
of three is better than that of one, if modernized,
would be, "The judgment of three is all-suffi-
cient."

Most of the nation's millionaires are godless.
There is no fear of God before their eyes; no
felt want of God in their hearts. They are flat-
tered, favored, and honored generally beyond
their intellectual and moral deserts. This is
their portion. We would not forget to note the
few noble exceptions to this rule. God has some
faithful stewards among the representatives of
great fortunes. Every week brings intelligence
of splendid gifts to worthy causes. But were all
the rich alike faithful to their trusts every hour
would include the present donations of seven
days.

What is true of the struggle for wealth is also
true of the pursuit of happiness. Indeed, the
same principles obtain throughout all depart-
ments of life. The five senses are depended

upon as the main channels for the reception of
life's coveted joys, and, as George MacDonald
tersely said, " The region of the senses is the un-
believing part of the human soul." The majority
never felt the thrill of highest happiness possible
to man. The little sensations of pleasure, conse-
quent upon agreeable taste, sight, or sound, are
naught compared with the exalted state of felicity to which the strong in Christ have attained.
To be strong is to be happy, and

> " True happiness ne'er entered at an eye ;
> True happiness resides in things unseen."

Nevertheless, the majority are well satisfied
with the pleasures of ungodliness, and appear
disinclined to distrust themselves, their fellows,
and the world for all the happiness they may
ever know.

Thus to one thing and another men devote all
their energies and powers. Their own mortality,
the limit of their endurance, and the brevity of
their career are lost sight of. Their one design—
to gratify self—is paramount above all others.
Such pray not, praise little, and humble themselves no more. The obligations of the creature
to the Creator they ignore. The dependence of
the finite upon the infinite they disregard. The

blessings of salvation they despise. Having entered upon life, they toil and strive, accumulate and enjoy, spend their strength with their years, grow gray, decrepit, weak, and childish, and at length gather up their weary feet and tremulously die, illustrating nothing more forcibly than the truth that all such strength is utter weakness, all such wisdom utter folly. What a contrast to such a life is that of the strong man in Christ! He liveth not to himself, and dieth not to himself. He lives with another life in view. While using the world he abuses it not. In health and strength and happiness he is thankful for such blessings. Remembering his Creator, he meets the obligations of the creature; appreciating the goodness of the Redeemer, he acts the obedient part of the redeemed; consecrating all to God, and using his gifts and faculties for the glory of God, he follows after purity, does good among men, is serene in spirit, resigned to the will of Heaven, awaits his call, hears the summons, and as he responds with his life, realizes, to his eternal joy, that God is the strength of his life and his portion forever.

IV.

FULL SURRENDER.

THE surrender of the will is the vital turning-point of the mind toward a life of piety and devotion to God.   But this surrender does not imply that the will shall no longer be actively exercised.   It is a mistake to imagine that the will of the Christian is no longer his own; that it lies inactive, as it were, a thing of disuse, and practically no longer needful.   The man of God is not such a machine as this false idea would make him.   It is true that he has submitted himself to God, that the spirit and cry of his heart is, "Not my will, but thine, O God, be done," yet he remains a man, with power to choose and to act as an enlightened conscience dictates; yea, more, with mental power to rebel against high Heaven, and to go back to a groveling life of sin and death.   The surrender of the will to God is nothing more or less than a sensible recognition of God's superior wisdom, power, and goodness, a desire to be subject unto him, and a resolute action of mind whereby all our powers are brought into harmony with God's laws as revealed in his word and by the influences of his Spirit. Our wills are not thus lost, except morally, to self and sin. They are still our own, though by their act we become God's children, with our wills subject unto his.

> " Our wills are ours, we know not how;
> Our wills are ours, to make them Thine."

Epictetus wrote, " There is nothing good or evil save in the will." A life of genuine holiness is not only a consistent life of faith in the Son of God, but a life of constant and conscious self-surrender of soul and body to his service. It is not enough that we once for a moment yielded ourselves to him; the yielding embraces a life-time of willing consecration. While by constant exercise the will becomes stronger in its inclination toward purity, and consequently weaker in its leaning toward the " filthiness of the flesh," yet every expression of a saintly life, whether in word, deed, or bearing, recognizable as a Christian trait, is the result of activity in the will, a deliberate choosing of right; in other words, a doing of the will of God. So steadfast and uniform may be these deliberations of the mind toward what is godlike, that a sort of habit of piety

is formed, and we speak of the happy subject as
a confirmed Christian, one established in the principles of a holy life.   It is thus seen that

> " The readiness of doing doth express
> No other but the doer's willingness."

It is his joy to do his Maker's will.   So complete is his self-mastery, under the power of
grace, that to live to God in Christ is his blessedness.   "I live!" he exclaims, "yet not I, but
Christ liveth in me."   "O what a blessed thing
it is," said Payson, "to lose one's will!   Since I
have lost my will I have found happiness.   There
can be no such thing as disappointment to me, for
I have no desires but that God's will may be accomplished."   This is the testimony of each one
who has found out what it is to give up his own
life, and to receive instead the blessed life of
Christ within him.

Thus Madame Guyon:

> " Peace has unveiled her smiling face,
> And woos thy soul to her embrace:
> Enjoyed with ease, if thou refrain
> From selfish love, else sought in vain;
> She dwells with all who truth prefer,
> But seeks not them who seek not her.
>
> " Yield to the Lord, with simple heart,
> All that thou hast, and all thou art;

Renounce all strength but strength divine,
And peace shall be forever thine;
Behold the path which I have trod,
My path, till I go home to God."

Abraham, when he pleaded with God for Sodom, felt himself to be "but dust and ashes;" and afterward, when called to give up his only son, Isaac, his answer, "Behold, here am I," indicated a willing, sincere mind, and an anxiety to know the will of God, that it might be obeyed. And we find in the Bible that this spirit characterizes the holiest men. Thus David declares, "Truly my soul waiteth upon God;" "My soul thirsteth after God;" "My soul breaketh for the longing that it hath unto his judgments at all times;" "How sweet are thy words unto my taste;" "Thy word is very pure, therefore thy servant loveth it;" "For thy sake are we killed all the day long;" "O how love I thy law." Isaiah cried, "Woe is me! for I am undone; for I am a man of unclean lips," etc.; and then, after the fire of God had touched his lips, he said, "Here am I; send me." Moses, at the manifestations of Jehovah, did "exceedingly fear and quake." Saul of Tarsus, trembling, said, "Lord, what wilt thou have me to do?" and afterward, at the thought of being a savor of life unto life unto

some, and of death unto death to others, he cried
out, "Who is sufficient for these things?" So
has it ever been when the Lord has subdued a
spirit by his grace. "To this man will I look,"
said he, "even to him that is poor, and of a con-
trite spirit, and trembleth at my word." The
least breath of the Spirit moves the true Christian, and his entire will vibrates to the pulsations
of love in the heart of Christ, the fountain head.

What God requires of us, declared the clear-
visioned Fénelon, is a will which is no longer di-
vided between him and any creature; a simple,
pliable state of will which desires what he desires, rejects nothing but what he rejects, and
wills without reserve what he wills, and under
no pretext wills what he does not. In this state
of mind all things are proper for us; our amusements even are acceptable in his sight.

Blessed is he who thus gives himself to God!
He is delivered from his passions, from the opin-
ions of men, from their malice, from the tyranny
of their maxims, from their cold and miserable
raillery, from the misfortunes which the world
attributes to chance, from the infidelity and fick-
leness of friends, from the artifices and snares of
enemies, from the wretchedness and shortness of
life, from the horrors of an ungodly death, from

the cruel remorse that follows sinful pleasures, and from the everlasting condemnation of God. Is not this worth while?   As the poet pleads:

> " O, soul! o'erwhelmed by grief and care,
> Come to thy God and bow in prayer;
> And know that every joy in one
> Is asked when breathed, 'Thy will be done.'
>
> " His will is best, his eyes can see
> Whate'er the future has for thee;
> Take neither joy nor grief alone,
> But say in each, 'Thy will be done.'
>
> " His will is often not like ours,
> Thorns seem to come instead of flowers;
> And rough may be the road to run,
> But, soul, still say, 'Thy will be done.'
>
> "Sometime, in realms of glittering gold,
> Where God each mystery shall unfold,
> We'll see 'twas best, when crowns we've won,
> That here we said, 'Thy will be done.' "

How many who have started in the Christian way have ascertained by a bitter experience that, in the matter of both entire surrender and simple trust, the greatest enemy is self. " Now it refuses to give up its will; then again, by its working, it hinders God's work. Unless this life of self, with its willing and working, be displaced by the life of Christ, with his willing and working, to abide in him will be impossible." It is

5

more dangerous to undertake to serve Christ selfishly than it is utterly to rebel against him. In the latter case there is little liability of self-deception, while in the former there may be a complacent dreaming of peace when there is no peace, and of a future heaven when there is preparation only for an endless hell.

We submit it as the most important step a man can take to voluntarily place himself in the attitude and experience of conscious self-surrender to God. The Bible requires it, and proclaims it as a condition of knowledge, usefulness, and heaven. "If any man will do his will, he shall know of the doctrine, whether it be of God." "If there be first a willing mind, it is accepted according to that a man hath." "He that doeth the will of God abideth forever." In one of our sacred songs the true sentiment is embodied:

> " My Jesus, as thou wilt:
>   O may thy will be mine;
> Into thy hand of love
>   I would my all resign.
> Through sorrow or through joy,
>   Conduct me as thine own,
> And help me still to say,
>   'My Lord, thy will be done.' "

A young clergyman of New York once wrote some lines on "The Consecrated Will," which

are very expressive, and ought to be better
known:

> " Laid on thine altar, O my Lord divine,
>   Accept my gift this day for Jesus' sake ;
> I have no jewels to adorn thy shrine,
>   Nor any world-famed sacrifice to make.
> But here I bring within my trembling hand
>   This will of mine—a thing that seemeth small ;
> And only thou, dear Lord, canst understand
>   How when I yield thee this I yield mine all.
> Hidden therein, thy searching eye can see
>   Struggles of passion, visions of delight,
> All that I love, or am, or fain would be—
>   Deep loves, fond hopes, and longings infinite.
> It hath been wet with tears and dimmed with sighs,
>   Clenched in my grasp, till beauty it hath none.
> Now from thy footstool, where it vanquished lies,
>   The prayer ascendeth, May thy will be done !
> Take it, O Father, ere my courage fail,
>   And merge it so in thine own will, that e'en
> If in some desperate hour my cries prevail,
>   And thou give back my gift, it may have been
> So changed, so purified, so fair have grown,
>   So one with thee, so filled with peace divine,
> I may not know or feel it as mine own,
>   But gaining back my will may find it thine."

V.

THE REVIVAL.

REVIVAL signifies a return to life, or a quick-
ening of life. It is a rising from a low state
into a higher. In religion it is the increase and
energizing of spiritual life, an extraordinary outpouring of God's power in the soul, and upon the
Church and the world.

Religious revivals are the life of the world.
As nature would die with continued winter, so
the world would utterly perish in wickedness if
God did not display his saving power. Who can
tell what history would have already recorded
but for the glorious reformation under Luther,
and the not less spiritual awakenings under Wesley, Whitefield, and Edwards?

Revivals often come unexpectedly to the multitude. The day of Pentecost was a surprise to
the Jews. The Church was very weak, and her
outlook apparently was unpromising enough.
Christ had been crucified, and had disappeared
from earth. Skepticism seemed to triumph.
The disciples were nearly disconsolate, but con-

tinued their prayers. At length the mysterious sound was heard, the cloven tongues appeared, the mighty power fell, and, endowed therewith, the apostles began publicly to preach and exhort, three thousand souls being saved the first day. But back of all this man's agency appears. Long days of waiting, watching, and application preceded the public spectacle. The world knew it not, but God and his faithful disciples knew.

For the salvation of souls great responsibility always devolves upon humanity. Some one has said that there never was a soul saved apart from human agency. Certain it is that God uses man to save man, and has sent his Spirit into the world for the very purpose of preparing it thoroughly for success in Christian work. "He [the Spirit] shall reprove the world of sin, of righteousness, and of judgment to come." When the unconverted are convicted of sin by the Holy Ghost it is the express mission of Christians to point them to Christ, to tenderly counsel them and lead them in the way of life. Nor are Christians always to wait for visible tokens of contrition. Serious hearts sometimes beat behind laughing faces. Some temperaments use this device to conceal godly sorrow. They sing when they feel like sighing, and smile when they can hardly refrain from tears.

Moreover, Christians cannot know just when their efforts for good will be most effectual. How often a single word spoken by a soul in communion with Christ is like the spark that springs a mine, opening up and clearing the way for the mighty revival which follows! No one can account for it. As a cause, it appears inadequate, but in the hands of God it is an earthquake shock, followed by a tremendous moral upheaval. We believe it might truthfully be said that in every case of genuine revival one or more souls have been dwelling in the inner sanctuary—have been waiting on the Lord for the renewal of strength—and thus invigorated, their simple words or deeds have inaugurated the visible manifestations of God's presence and power. It is somewhere written that a poor blacksmith in western New York became greatly concerned for the state of the Church. Unable either to work or rest, he closed his shop and betook himself to prayer. There were no doubts or misgivings in his heart as he wrestled mightily for the spirit and power of revival in the Churches. At length a meeting was opened. God's Spirit came upon the people. The fire of love began to burn.

The faith of many was strengthened and their spiritual life quickened. The influence extended to the unconverted, and, ere the meeting closed, over two hundred souls were saved. What a triumph for the humble blacksmith; and what a beautiful illustration of the truth that God is no respecter of persons: but in every nation and in every place he that feareth him, and worketh righteousness, is accepted with him!

There are three agencies to be depended upon for the promotion of revivals—the word of God, the work of the Spirit, and the labors of Christians. The first two are the same to-day as when Whitefield and Edwards became instrumental in turning thousands to God. The success of Moody and other great evangelists proves that the super-human agencies are as effectual as ever. How is it with the remaining instrumentality? We well know that when these three agencies operate in concert revivals follow. Sinners cannot resist the combined influence of proclaimed Bible truth, moving Spirit-power, and active Christian faith and work. They may resist any two of them, but not all. Now, the word and Spirit are always testifying to the truth, but Christians, the only remaining agency, so speak and act, or fail to speak and act, as to nullify their influences.

"Ye are our epistles," said the apostle, "known and read of all men." What do sinners read of us? Is it the spirit and temper, the meekness and gentleness, the humility and lowliness, the self-denial and charity, the zeal and activity of Jesus Christ? Do we set no examples of unbelief, selfishness, worldliness, and folly? Have not our lives, if not our lips, been testifying against the blessed agencies of God's word and Spirit? And have not sinners by thousands believed our testimony and unfortunately rejected God and Christ?

Genuine brotherly love is promotive of the revival spirit, but how little of it there is in the world! Most Christians, and worldlings, too, can say, "I have nothing against any of my brethren," which is about equivalent to, "I do not now downrightly hate any of them." True brotherly love is characterized by a tender sympathy with and lively interest in the welfare of fellow-Christians. It is such a spirit as Christ exercised toward them in offering himself a sacrifice for them, after he had gone about healing their diseases, comforting their hearts, and doing them good in every possible way. Where this spirit is exemplified in the Church the unconverted look on, know that it is different from the spirit of the world, that it is the right spirit, a spirit to be desired and promoted, and straightway they feel a new interest in the grace of Christ which begets it. This is the beginning of a revival.

In every community there are persons whose lives are outwardly circumspect, who are respectful toward the Church and the ministry—nay, more, are liberal supporters of them, contributing of their substance and personally attending the public services—who, after all, are unrenewed in the spirit of their minds, and no nearer the kingdom of God to-day than they were ten years ago. They are the class whom Paul designated as " ever learning, yet never coming to a knowledge of the truth." There is some essential lack in the Church when the unsaved can thus continue on from one decade to another, no break ever being made in their ranks by sound conversion to Christ. How often it has occurred that when a community is visited with a gracious outpouring of the Spirit such persons are happily rescued! Only a breath from heaven can do it. They are proof against logical preaching and telling conversational argument. Prayer and exhortation under the regular routine affect them not. It must be a message from the throne, em-

phasized by the infinite energies of the Holy
Ghost, to break such hearts and build them up in
God.

Yet humanity is to do all it can. Men are
to go to the very extremity of their ability ere
expecting that God shall come to the rescue.
When ministers lay their time, talents, affections,
energies anew upon the altar, making a complete
sacrifice of themselves and their all for the Master's use; when laymen follow their examples, and
come up to the help of the Lord against the
mighty, the world is generally presented with a
spectacle of conquest and victory wonderful to
behold.

As a rule there needs to be a general confession
as well as forsaking of sin before a great outpouring of the Spirit may be expected. "We
have sinned with our fathers, and have done
wickedly." There never was a period when the
disposition to self-indulgence and palliation for
wickedness was so strong as to-day. The prevailing concession seems to be, "We are all poor,
miserable sinners, none better than the masses,
and we all stand or fall together." Never was
there a more fatal error. Every man answereth
for himself. There is a narrow way in which we
may walk and find heaven at last, even though

the broad way be thronged with travelers to destruction. The trouble is, people have a lurking desire for self-indulgence, if not for the commission of some secret sin, and this is why they talk about the necessity of sinning and attempt to justify it. It will not do. God is holy, and doth not look upon sin with allowance. We must confess our sins and forsake them, else salvation is impossible, and it may be said that no sin is truly confessed which is not forsaken. We must loathe unrighteousness in our inmost souls, and we must confess with the mouth, as well as the life, that others shall know that the spirit of holiness is born within us. This will give us power. We have no confidence in our prayers when our hearts condemn us. We do not and cannot expect God to answer them. But when our hearts are broken — when we have confessed and put away all our sins—our confidence will be great in asking, and no needed blessing will be withheld.

Spurgeon well says, "Let the bucket of the heart be turned upside down and drained of the love of sin, and then prayer will be heard and Jesus will come in and fill it."

"Bring ye all the tithes into the store-house, that there may be meat in mine house, and prove me now herewith, saith the Lord of hosts, if I will not open the windows of heaven, and pour you out a blessing, that there shall not be room enough to receive it." God has put a close connection also between Christian beneficence and spiritual power, between the meeting of our financial obligations as Churches and individuals and the outpouring of revival mercy. Jesus preached most powerfully against the sin of covetousness, and one of the first results of the outpouring of the Spirit on the day of Pentecost was generous gifts of money—in some cases "whole possessions"—to form a common treasury for the apostles' use. The people of the early Churches "first gave themselves to the Lord," and then out of their "deep poverty" devised liberal things. Too many people of modern Churches fail, even out of immense riches, to bestow just offerings for the promotion of God's work. They need not go beyond this fact for the secret of the barrenness which attends protracted meetings. The "windows of heaven" are not open to such as bring not the tithes. Prayers, exhortations, and other spiritual services are good, but there must also be a touch of the same grace that was in Christ, "who, though he was rich, yet for our sakes became poor." We must have his spirit of sacrifice and self-denial. It is thus we live in him and he in us. A common spirit begets a common sympathy and a common life.

" If ye abide in me," says Jesus, " and my words abide in you, ye shall ask what ye will, and it shall be done unto you." Too many remember this promise but forget its condition, whereas the condition is the vital point they should fix in their hearts. " To the Christian who is not abiding wholly in Jesus, the difficulty of asking blessings, and perhaps receiving them not, is so great as to rob him of the comfort and the strength it could bring. Under the guise of humility, he asks how one so unworthy could expect to have influence with the holy One. He prays, but it is more because he cannot rest without prayer than from a loving faith that the prayer will be heard. But what a blessed relief from such perplexity is given to the man who is truly abiding in Christ! He realizes increasingly how it is in the real spiritual unity with Christ that we are accepted and heard. The union with the Son of God is a life union: we are in very deed one with him—our prayer ascends as his prayer, our offering is accepted as his offering. It is because we abide in him in constant devotedness and self-denying generosity that we can ask what we will and it is given us. Such a state inclines us to pray according to the will of God, and with the purpose of seeking only his glory. It works in us the faith which alone can obtain the answer and keep us in the place where the answer can be bestowed."

Under such conditions the active, praying spirit is not sufficiently alive in the Church. We have grown rich and increased with goods, and have come to think that we need nothing, and others need nothing from us, forgetting that we have the poor always with us, and that morally we are as ever destitute, poor, and blind, having the same seeds of death in our natures, and exposed, as of old, to banishment from God and eternal misery. In the aggregate there is considerable paying, but very little real sacrifice for pure love's sake. There is much formal praying, but little of the wrestling that prevails with God and secures the blessing. This is the reason why doubt has sprung up as to the efficacy of prayer. The best way, the only way, to dissolve the doubt is by personal consecration of all we have to God, and by living communion with him. While cold-hearted skepticism may reason and deny, warm-hearted, brother-loving faith is persevering in effort and prevailing in prayer for that grandeur of victory and fullness of blessing which only the consciously saved enjoy. O for more of this earnest, confident, prevailing prayer! O for more of this self-denying and self-giving spirit of service! How they would energize the weakened forces of the Church and change the attitude and spirit of worldly men! Numerous, remarks another, as are the ranks of the unconverted, they will most surely and rapidly disappear when once the passion of saving souls takes possession of Christ's Church on earth; when, in the warehouse and in the shop, in the factory and in the mill, in the granary and in the field, on the roadside and at the fireside, in the city and in the country, on the sea and on the shore, men and women are eagerly watching to win some soul to Christ; when love for the world shall burn in each heart, prayer for the world ascend from each lip, bounty for the world drop from each hand, the message gush from every tongue; then, O then, shall linger no longer the salvation of a ruined race!

VI.

THE CHRISTIAN SPIRIT.

HOW familiar the expression, "You must show a Christian spirit;" or, "That is not the Christian spirit." What is meant by it?

Were any one trait of character or disposition to be selected as the exponent of the Christian spirit, that of gentleness or tenderness would most likely meet the common view. According to this notion, all harshness of speech and severity of measures would be condemned as not in keeping with the Christian spirit. Let any one quality be chosen to represent that spirit, and numerous other qualities would fall under censure.

What is the Christian spirit? We answer, No one quality can represent it under all circumstances. It is not kindness simply, nor gentleness, nor patience, nor forgiveness, though any of these graces may exhibit it in certain relations. It is not resignation only, nor humility, but it is that condition of mind and heart which is suited to the circumstances in which one providentially may be placed. "Under injuries, for example, meekness is a Christian spirit; under intense personal suffering, patience is a Christian spirit; toward a wrong-doer who is penitent, forgiveness is a Christian spirit." And so on to the end of all the traits of Christian character and life.

There come times in the history of individuals when much firmness and decision are necessary to the maintenance of Christian character. Under such circumstances a yielding, acquiescing spirit would be any thing but Christian. An illustration is found in Dr. Mahan's account of the daughter of an English nobleman who providentially was brought under the influence of deeply religious people, and thus came to a saving knowledge of the truth as it is in Jesus. The father was almost distracted at the event, and by threats, temptations to extravagance in dress, by reading and traveling in foreign countries, and to places of fashionable resort, took every means in his power to divert her mind from "things unseen and eternal." But her "heart was fixed." The God of Abraham had become "her shield, and her exceeding great reward," and she was determined that nothing finite should deprive her of her infinite and eternal portion in him or displace him from the center of her heart. At last the father

6

resolved upon a final and desperate expedient, by
which his end should be gained, or his daughter
ruined, so far as her prospects in this life were
concerned. A large company of the nobility
were invited to his house. It was so arranged
that, during the festivities, the daughters of different noblemen, and among others this one,
were to be called on to entertain the company
with singing and music on the piano. If she
complied, she parted with heaven and returned
to the world; if she refused compliance, she
would be publicly disgraced, and lose, past the
possibility of recovery, her place in society. It
was a dreadful crisis, and with peaceful confidence did she await it. As the crisis approached
different individuals, at the call of the company,
performed their parts with the greatest applause.
At last the name of this daughter was announced.
In a moment all were in fixed and silent suspense
to see how the scale of destiny would turn.
Without hesitation she rose, and with a calm and
dignified composure took her place at the instrument. After a moment spent in silent prayer,
she ran her fingers along the keys, and then, with
an unearthly sweetness, elevation, and solemnity,
sang, accompanying her voice with the notes of
the instrument, the following stanzas:

"No room for mirth or trifling here,
For worldly hope, or worldly fear,
　　If life so soon is gone;
If now the Judge is at the door,
And all mankind must stand before
　　The inexorable throne!

"No matter which my thoughts employ,
A moment's misery or joy;
　　But O! when both shall end,
Where shall I find my destined place?
Shall I my everlasting days
　　With fiends, or angels spend?

"Nothing is worth a thought beneath,
But how I may escape the death
　　That never, never dies;
How make mine own election sure;
And, when I fail on earth, secure
　　A mansion in the skies.

"Jesus, vouchsafe a pitying ray;
Be thou my guide, be thou my way
　　To glorious happiness.
Ah! write the pardon on my heart,
And whensoe'er I hence depart,
　　Let me depart in peace."

The minstrel ceased. The solemnity of eternity was upon that assembly. Without speaking they dispersed. The father wept aloud, and when left alone sought the counsel and prayers of his daughter for the salvation of his soul.

His soul was saved, and his great estate consecrated to Christ.

In the wisdom which selected that hymn for
such an occasion, and the hallowed and sweet
manner of its utterance, we have a full realization of all that is embraced in the Christian spirit
under the trying circumstances named. And so
the individual who, according to his best knowledge and judgment, does as God requires, no
matter how placed, manifests a Christian spirit.
The pious Fletcher would term it that recollected
state of mind which guards the lips, controls the
countenance, molds the expression, moves the
limbs, girds the loins, and, in a word, brings into
subserviency to Christ the demeanor, the walk,
the habits, the very instincts of the being.

Such a definition of the Christian spirit nullifies
the notion that it is confined to the softer traits
of the religious life. Christians are sometimes
placed in circumstances in which rebuke, not forgiveness, exposure, not submission, are absolutely
demanded. Meekness would be entirely out of
place in a Christian knowingly related to another
professor who was persisting in a course of hei-
nous offense against virtue and decency. The
spirit of abhorrence, or even of denunciation, is
sometimes quite as much a Christian spirit as in

other relations that of forbearance and long-suffering would be.

But the public mind may not be as ready to pass favorable sentence upon a stern, harsh exhibition of character as upon a quiet, placable trait. And it must be remembered that the sterner traits of Christianity are always to be tempered with the gentler. The Christian must bear about with him the spirit of the Lord Jesus, who, when he was reviled, reviled not again, in the same appropriate way as when, on another occasion, he drove the traders from the temple and overthrew the tables of the money-changers.

It is said of a certain great religious leader that he once came in contact with the wealthy proprietor of an estate who was in fearful rage at a slave standing before him and trembling on account of a sentence, the execution of which was to him far more dreadful than death. The distinguished man besought the slave-holder to forgive the wrong. "Never," was the haughty reply; "when I receive an injury I never forgive it." "Then," was the fitting reply, "I trust you yourself have never committed a sin or done a wrong." Like a sudden flash from the pyre of the last judgment these words shot to the heart of the angry man. A sinner like himself to adopt the maxim never to forgive! Conviction of his error seized upon him, and, with a subdued spirit, he pardoned the helpless offender, and apologized to his visitor. Who fails to recognize the Christian spirit in the wise and mild rebuke which was so effective and so richly deserved? Had it been worded less happily, or administered in an austere manner, no doubt the rich man's pride and combativeness would have been aroused and visited with redoubled fury upon the slave and contempt upon the reprover.

Paul was in some respects a splendid example of the Christian spirit. He was prepared to become all things to all men if by any means he might save some. To the Philippian jailer he was a son of consolation, but to the Roman governor a son of thunder. In the one case he was quick to sympathize and direct in the way of peace; in the other bold to denounce and even to expose reasoning with all the vehemence of his impetuous nature upon the very themes which cut Felix to the heart and lay bare his sins to the torture of his own quickened conscience.

Melanchthon, amiable and gentle as he was, showed no more of the true Christian spirit than did Luther, who, like a stern warrior, resolved to drive pope and cardinals to the wall and liberate

the world from the thralldom of priestly assump-
tion. The minister who rebukes sinners and tries
unruly members may not be as calmly judged as
the one who lets the deluded sleep on to their
own destruction, but in the sight of God he
shows more of the Christian spirit. Every true
reformer exposes himself to harsh judgment, but
he must be prepared to say with Paul, "With me
it is a small matter that I should be judged of
you, or of man's judgment; he that judgeth me
is the Lord."

Our blessed Lord himself was accused of having "a devil"—an unchristian spirit—and it is
enough that the servant be as his Lord. But let
us not be misunderstood. A spirit of censorious-
ness, agitation, harshness, and so forth, may be
decidedly unchristian. We need to be wise as
serpents and harmless as doves. It is the bane
of some that they confound the most solemn dis-
tinctions, and lack in a culpable degree the faculty of discernment. We should study the mind
of Christ and keep before us the truth that while
severity or indignation may sometimes be appropriately conspicuous, yet it will ever be surrounded
with "a galaxy of heavenly virtues, in whose
sweet light it will appear a vastly different
thing from that bitter severity or fierce indig-

nation with which the mere moralist castigates vice."

The psalmist prayed, " Renew a right spirit within me." The Christian spirit is a right spirit. Its characteristics have been delineated as, first, a spirit of supreme love to God and universal love to man. It implies the absence of all revenge, hatred, or enmity toward any creature. A right spirit is a humble spirit, inclined to misgiving and self-distrust. It is a tender spirit, always ready to feel for others, and prompt to bestow aid. A right spirit is a cheerful, hopeful spirit, that never yields to doubt or despondency. It is resigned to the will of God and complacent in all his dealings. It is benevolent and generous in the use of temporal means, but at the same time provident and prudent in all temporal interests. A right spirit is devout and watchful and full of solicitude for the salvation of men. It is a spirit of contentment, rejoicing in the blessings of a beneficent Providence, meek under reproaches, and patient under all afflictions and trials. The power of a right spirit is beyond conception. It impresses all who come in contact with it. A man may resist argument and disdain reproof, but a right spirit will finally subdue the hardest heart.*

* Rev. J. M. Arnold, D.D.

The Christian spirit is a right spirit in relation to the Church. It recognizes the Church as a divinely established means for propagating truth and spreading righteousness abroad. It identifies itself with the Church, is zealous for the honor of the Church, and does all within its power to sustain the Church in her enterprises.

By the Church, we mean any truly evangelical Church, or the general spirit of them all. We institute no plea for sectarian amalgamation. No doubt there are too many denominations. No use of a separate Church for every human whim. No reason, for instance, why there should be in this country a half dozen Methodist bodies, different sects of Baptists, and several Presbyterian branches. A measure of consolidation would be a boon. But society requires the characteristic features of several denominations. Something of variety is God's order in grace as well as in nature. A trinity in unity is the essential nature of the Godhead. And this is precisely the idea Jesus intended to convey when he prayed, "That they all may be one; as thou, Father, art in me, and I in thee, that they also may be one in us: that the world may believe that thou hast sent me." John xvii, 21. It is a perversion of Scripture to make this passage imply a consolidation of all the Churches. Jamieson, Fausset, and Brown, in their notes, say: "The unity of Christ's disciples must be something that shall be visible or perceptible to the world. What is it, then? Not certainly a merely formal, mechanical unity of ecclesiastical machinery. For as that may, and to a large extent does, exist in both the Western and Eastern Churches, with little of the Spirit of Christ—yea, much, much with which the Spirit of Christ cannot dwell—so, instead of convincing the world beyond its own pale of the divinity of the Gospel, it generates infidelity to a large extent within its own bosom. But the Spirit of Christ, illuminating, transforming, and reigning in the hearts of the genuine disciples of Christ, drawing them to each other as members of one family, and prompting them to loving co-operation for the good of the world—this is what, when sufficiently glowing and extended, shall force conviction upon the world that Christianity is divine. Doubtless, the more that differences among Christians disappear—the more they can agree even in minor matters—the impression upon the world may be expected to be greater. But it is not dependent upon this; for living and loving oneness in Christ is sometimes more touchingly seen even amid and in spite of minor differences than where no such differences exist to try the strength of their deeper unity. Yet till this living brotherhood in Christ shall show itself strong enough to destroy the sectarianism, selfishness, carnality, and apathy that eat out the heart of Christianity in all the visible sections of it, in vain shall we expect the world to be overawed by it. It is when 'the Spirit shall be poured upon us from on high,' as a Spirit of truth and love, and upon all parts of the Christian territory alike, melting down differences and heart-burnings, kindling astonishment and shame at past unfruitfulness, drawing forth longings of catholic affection, and yearning over a world lying in wickedness, embodying themselves in palpable forms and active measures—it is then that we may expect the effect here announced to be produced, and then it will be irresistible. Should not Christians ponder these things? Should not the same mind be in them which was also in Christ Jesus about this matter? Should not his prayer be theirs?"

Dr. Whedon rightfully observes that already "amid every diversity there is among true Christians a true unity." "The attempt has been made to bring the Christian body under one human head—the pope—and what has been the result? The head became ambitious, corrupt, despotic, infidel, and bloody. This was substituting for God's unity of the Spirit man's unity of temporal power."

The spiritual unity of evangelical denominations grows stronger every year. Sectarian differences that have long hindered universal Christian fellowship are rapidly sinking out of sight. While they may not entirely disappear in one generation, they will, we trust, get out of the way of such an exhibition of world-wide Christian love and endeavor that the unregenerated every-where will feel most powerfully the saving presence of Christ in the Churches.

It would be a wise measure if the several denominations would appoint a commission to determine what principles shall obtain among local churches, especially in newer towns and city suburbs, as to the occupancy of territory and the organization of societies. These matters rarely amicably adjust themselves. There must be some way of solving the perplexing problems.

Proselytism is a practice that should now, henceforth, and forever cease. It is of the spirit of the devil, not of Christ. Proselyters are blind. They see not that Christ's cause gains absolutely nothing by their efforts, however successful, but often suffers irreparable loss. There is not one spark of the true Christian spirit in a proselyting preacher. He is a wolf in sheep's clothing.

The Christian spirit is a right spirit in relation to the world. It recognizes what is good in man, what is desirable in life, and what is worth effort to accomplish or possess. It uses the world as not abusing it. It does not withdraw from it because it is wicked, but stays in it to work for it and make it better. It does not despair of the world because it persists in sin and in rejecting Christ, but endeavors to show it a more excellent way, and to prevail upon it to be reconciled to God. It does not proclaim religion as a penance, something simply to be endured in reference to future enjoyment, but practically illustrates how religion is to be enjoyed now, the happiest life to live, and the sweetest death to die. True religion is joyous, and is best manifested by a joyous spirit. When Philip preached Christ in Samaria there was " great joy in that city."

Sour complaints and long faces are no elements of genuine Christianity. They are of the earth, earthy. Yet we are told that Jesus never laughed. This is probably an inference drawn from the Bible statement that he " wept." The mission of Jesus to earth was grave indeed. Knowing what was in man, and conscious of the bloody baptism awaiting him when he had accomplished the work given him to do, it is not strange that a tinge of sadness is found in his utterances and in the record of his life. But we believe that Jesus often smiled. He blessed his fond mother by his innocent glee when an infant in her arms. In his boyhood, though thoughtful and pure, he grew in favor with many a charmed circle. In manhood he was pleasant while profound, and gentle while severe. He often told his followers to rejoice. Martyrs have sung and laughed while the flames consumed their bodies; so he who was led as a lamb to the slaughter felt the movings of an inward joy, the joy that was set before him while he endured the cross. Like unto his is the spirit of the Christian. It is never frivolous or trifling, but is always pleasant aud deeply in earnest. It sees for fallen man but one hope, and proclaims that that hope once lost is lost forever, but, laid hold upon, it proves the soul's sure anchor, entering into that within the veil.

VII.

UNFALTERING TRUST.

NO state of mind is more delightful than that of entire confidence in the providence of God. It gives contentment to the mind, repose to the spirit, and satisfaction to the heart. When we sleep an Eye that never slumbers watches over us. When we wake an ever-present Spirit marks our pathway. In time of need a divine Hand supplies our wants. In temptation he succors us, and in trial he sympathizes with us, and sends such relief as is for our good. In all God's dealings and ways the trusting soul is led to rejoice. "It will be such weather as pleases me to-morrow," said the Shepherd of Salisbury Plain, "because it will be such weather as pleases God."

Cecil pondered over the reverent expression of Rutherford, "I lay my head to rest on the bosom of Omnipotence," and declared that while he could keep such a thought uppermost in his mind it would always be a fine day whether it rained, hailed, or shone.

"O holy trust! O endless sense of rest!
　　Like the beloved John
To lay his head upon the Saviour's breast,
　　And thus to journey on."

"I have long seemed to be leaning on God alone, with no earthly prop to sustain me," wrote a devoted young Christian lady, whose hold on the world had been loosened by suffering, and whose experience had taught her that the earthly and temporal are very uncertain. "If, in his wisdom," she continued, "he raises up one and another to comfort and support, it is he that does it, so that I still lean on him alone. The Lord grant that it may ever be thus. I would live in no other way if I could than by faith, daily faith in God; nor receive any blessing or comfort or favor that I could not directly trace to him as bestowed in answer to prayer. It is a blessed way to live. Strange that I could not have found it out before. But we are stupid to learn what is for our own best interest, and probably I should not had it not been beaten into me by the rod—a rod of love. Yet since I have in some measure learned the lesson, I have longed that others should learn it also—those who have known something of God, and those who have not; to cast all care on the Lord, believing that he cares for us, and is infinitely more concerned for our happiness than we ourselves. O my heart breaks when I think how we have overlooked this thing—that God does care for us, and is striving to promote our happiness in every possible way, yet we have not believed it, and have therefore taken it into our hands to secure it, as though infinite wisdom and benevolence and power could not and would not secure it better than ourselves. O fools, and slow of heart to believe! My brothers, can you believe this truth? and will you from this time leave yourselves and all you have with God, and, seeking to know and do his will, let him take care of your interests and your happiness? Be assured that he will; and, indeed, in no other way can they be secured, for he that seeketh his life shall lose it, and he that loseth it for Christ's sake the same shall find it."

Dr. Henry A. Reynolds, the celebrated "Red Ribbon" reformer, writing in view of a recent severe affliction, makes known the source of his support in these words, "I believe that were it not for the unbounded confidence I have that God knows what is best for me, I should be an insane man."

God knows what is best for every human being, but unhappily only a few learn this blessed truth,

7

and anchor themselves and all their interests
to it.

We are inclined to believe, with Rev. Dr. O.
H. Warren, that to many believers "the sweet
surrender of earthly things to the care of their
Lord is more difficult than to trust him with their
more precious spiritual interests. They have
learned to commit their souls to the keeping of
his loving heart with an undoubting confidence;
but when they look at their present temporal
needs, the claims of their dependent loved ones,
the uncertainties of business, the probability of
sickness or disability, and the bitterness of possible poverty, they become a prey to that gnawing
anxiety, which is worse than most of the evils
they apprehend. They invite care, that hateful
bird of evil omen, to perch on the desks of their
counting-rooms, and even on the gas-brackets in
their chambers. They gaze so intently on the
visage of this disgusting bird that they fail to
hear the sweet voice of the Master earnestly
whispering, 'Your heavenly Father knoweth that
ye have need of these things . . . all these things
shall be added unto you. Take therefore no
[anxious] thought for the morrow.' Would they
give believing heed to these whispers they would
speedily drive care out of their windows and feel

as sure that Christ cares for their earthly well-being as they do that he will keep their souls safe from the power of the evil one."

How inconsistent with the belief that God sustains to us the endearing relation of Father and Benefactor is this slavery to carking care. Do we not belie our profession and incur the guilt of sinful distrust when we worry over business affairs and temporal engagements, which, at longest, can be ours but for a brief period, and which are ours only for practical usefulness? "Be anxious for nothing," for food, drink, and raiment, or any earthly interest, however dear.

This is far from suggesting that we are not to engage in earthly work at all, nor do our part in caring for our bodies. It is worse than infidelity not to look after our own. Diligence in business is quite as much enjoined as fervency of spirit in the Lord's service. The point is that all our service should be the Lord's, and in it we are diligently to exercise our powers. God gave us our bodies as well as our souls, and he is pleased to have us moderately feed the one that we may work out the salvation of the other. Work and worry are very different things.

Men are sometimes placed in situations in which strong confidence in God is their only stay. They are beyond the reach of human help, yet, if they accomplish their mission, they must stand their ground and battle on, however the victory seems for the time being to turn.

"Permit us to labor on in obscurity, and in twenty years you may hear from us again," was the report of the pious Judson to the American Churches after several years of apparently fruitless missionary labor in Burmah. "Do you think the prospects bright for the conversion of the heathen?" was asked of him. "As bright," replied the confiding servant of Christ, "as bright as the promises of God." It was just such a spirit of strong confidence in God which led David to exclaim, "I have set thy law always before me; because he is at my right hand I shall not be moved." "He only is my rock and my salvation: he is my defense, I shall not be greatly moved." The good man, doing his Maker's will, knows no discouragements nor fears. He

> "lays his hand upon the sky,
> Then bids earth roll, nor heeds her idle whirl."

He trusts in God because he has an enlightened conception of the greatness and goodness of the divine character. He recognizes in God pre-eminent ability and disposition to protect and defend him, to guide him aright, and to give him a proper measure of success. In his every-day life and work he does not look upon God as afar off. He knows that he is nigh, even in the heart. He is never less alone than when, in his closet, he feels the presence of the Father, Son, and Holy Ghost, sweetly in their various offices drawing him into more perfect fellowship and richer communion. He studies the Bible and hears the divine voice in the inspired page, saying, " The words that I speak unto you, they are spirit and they are life." He drinks in the spirit of the book. To him all its truths are real, and deeply felt. Looking up, he exclaims with one of old, " Thy word have I hid in my heart, that I might not sin against thee." " O how I love thy law: it is my meditation all the day."

In times of trouble and sorrow his trust is unshaken. Bowing submissively to the stroke, he acknowledges the authority of the Hand that smites. He knows there is no other ground of consolation. His spirit and language are:

> " Thou art, O Lord, my only trust,
> When friends are mingled with the dust,
>   And all my loves are gone.
> When earth has nothing to bestow,
> And every flower is dead below,
>   I look to thee alone.

" Thou wilt not leave, in doubt and fear,
The humble soul who loves to hear
   The lessons of thy word.
When foes around us thickly press,
And all is danger and distress,
   There's safety in the Lord.

" The bosom friend may sleep below
The church-yard turf, and we may go
   To close a loved one's eyes:
They will not always slumber there;
We see a world more bright and fair,
   A home beyond the skies.

" 'Tis thou, O Lord, who shield'st my head,
And draw'st thy curtains round my bed;
   I sleep secure in thee.
And, O, may soon that time arrive,
When we before thy face shall live,
   Through all eternity."—PERCIVAL.

Pleasant and delightful, indeed, is such a spirit of continued commerce with God, according to the league and covenant struck with him.

"To be a friend of God, an associate of the Most High, a domestic, no more a stranger, a foreigner, but of his own household; to live wholly upon the plentiful provisions, and under the happy order and government of his family; to have a heart to seek all from him, and lay out all for him. How great is the pleasure of trust, of living free from care; that is, of any thing but

how to please and honor him in a cheerful and
unsolicitous dependence, expecting from him our
daily bread, believing that he will not let our
souls famish; that while they hunger and thirst
after righteousness, they shall be filled; that they
shall be sustained with the bread and water of
life; that when they hunger he will feed them
with hidden manna, and with the fruits that grow
on the tree of life in the midst of the paradise of
God; that when they thirst he will give water,
and add milk and honey without money and without price; and for the body, not to doubt that he
that feeds ravens and clothes lilies will feed and
clothe them. To be so taken up in seeking his
kingdom and righteousness, as freely to leave it
to him to add the other things as he sees fit—to
take no thought for the morrow—to have a heart
framed herein according to divine precept; not
to be encumbered or kept in anxious suspense by
the thoughts or fears of what may fall out, by
which many suffer the same affliction a thousand
times over, which God would have them suffer
but once—a firm repose on the goodness of providence, and its firm and unerring wisdom; a steady
persuasion that our heavenly Father knows what
we have need of, and what is fittest for us to
want, to suffer, or enjoy. How delightful a life

do these make! and how agreeable to one born
of God, his own son, and heir of all things, as
being joint heirs with Christ, and claiming by
that large grant that says 'all things are yours,'
only that in minority it is better to have a wise
Father's allowance than to be your own carvers."
—HOWE.

Such a spirit implies a deep sense of dependence on God, and little or no dependence on any
other source of defense and consolation. It sees
how full the Divine hand is of blessing, how far
extended the Divine arm is to save. It recognizes
human weakness, ignorance, and unfaithfulness.
It perceives the truth of Christ's own words: "He
that abideth in me, and I in him, the same bringeth forth much fruit; for without me ye can do
nothing." We must go directly to God, and
there abide, deriving from him pardon, peace,
sanctification, redemption, and the entire support
of our spiritual life. In him we have a fountain
always full.

> "Its streams the whole creation reach,
>   So plenteous is the store;
> Enough for all, enough for each,
>   Enough for evermore."

In the trusting heart religion becomes a deep
stream, always flowing, and whose current is

peaceful and strong. The channel is always full,
because an exhaustless fountain feeds it. God is
the source of its supply, and the stream partakes
of his purity and unchangeableness. It is not at
one time a destructive torrent, and at another a
stagnant pool. It is permanent life and perpetual
blessing. It is a complete fulfillment of the promise, "Whosoever drinketh of the water that I
shall give him shall never thirst; but the water
that I shall give him shall be in him a well of
water springing up into everlasting life." "The
Spirit of God descends into the heart, and sup-
ports the spiritual life, much as the dews and
rains of heaven support vegetable life." The
trusting heart drinks in this Holy Spirit. It is
baptized with it. The Spirit is the source of all
its sweet peace, its holy joy, its exulting emotions,
its practical godliness. It does not depend on
outward impulses, on external causes. It lives
directly on God, and draws from him all its holy
energy, its vital principle, its living, moving
power.

For every individual there exist fountains of
exhaustless blessedness in God, but they are
fountains sealed until confiding trust brings the
soul near to them, and pure love begins to flow
out from his own heart toward all beings in need

of sympathy and capable of happiness. Then these fountains are opened, and, uniting in their flow, the river of life pours its broad streams into the soul. The desert place is thus made glad. The flowers of hope spring up, and the fruits of the Spirit abound. Somebody has said that it is better to be in hell with love, than to be in heaven without it. It is better to be in trouble and danger and suffering, with confidence in God, than to be in carnal happiness and security without it.

"I remember," says Rev. Dr. C. H. Fowler, " standing by the surging billows all one weary day, and watching for hours a father struggling beyond in the breakers for the life of his son. They came slowly toward the shore on a piece of wreck, and as they came, the waves turned over the piece of float, and they were lost to view. Suddenly we saw the father come to the surface and clamber alone to the wreck, and then saw him plunge off into the waves, and thought he was gone; but in a moment he came back bringing his boy. Presently they struck another wave, and over they went; and again repeated the process. Again they went over, and again the father rescued his son. By and by, as they swung nearer the land, they caught on a snag, just out beyond where we could reach them, and for a little time the waves went over them till we saw the boy in the father's arms, hanging down in helplessness, and knew they must be saved soon or be lost. I shall never forget the gaze of that father. As we drew him from the devouring waves, still clinging to his son, he said, 'That's my boy! that's my boy!' And so I have thought, in the hours of darkness, when the billows roll over me, the great Father reaching down to me, and taking hold of me, crying, 'That's my boy!' and I know I am safe."

God loves the trusting heart, and the trusting heart loves God. They that dwell in love must, in every state and condition, dwell in God; for God is love.

VIII.

SPIRITUAL VISION.

IT is a mistake for the irreligious man to suppose that he understands religion. A heathen in the jungles of Africa might as well think that he is acquainted with civilization. Locke tells of a blind man who thought that the color of scarlet was like the sound of a bell. The blind man was not a fool, but there was a serious defect in his eye. Had he possessed the power of vision, and used it rightly, he would have reached a correct conclusion.

The unregenerate are incompetent to pass judgment upon religious truth and life. They have never had their eyes opened. Without being destitute of the power of vision, "their eyes they have closed; lest . . . they should see with their eyes, and . . . understand with their heart." They have never perceived and felt the truth. They seeing see not, and it is not given unto them to know the mysteries of the spiritual kingdom. Whatever strength of mind they may have, they are disqualified to judge respecting evangelical religion, for they know nothing about it. The truth is, the natural man, no matter how high his place in the world's intellectual enlightenment, is but half developed. The things of the Spirit, which constitute more than half of the richest experiences of a perfected human life, all lie beyond his ken. The great apostle affirmed that "the natural man receiveth not the things of the Spirit of God: for they are foolishness unto him: neither can he know them, because they are spiritually discerned." The Christian has an unmistakable realization of a world of truth and life, which is as completely hidden from the unsaved as are the magnificent scientific developments of our own age and land to the untutored savage in his hut of ice amid the polar seas.

The prophet Elisha was once surrounded by the Syrian army, sent on purpose to take him. To human appearance there was no way of escape. His servant was alarmed, and exclaimed, "Alas, my master! how shall we do? . . . And Elisha prayed, and said, Lord, I pray thee, open his eyes, that he may see. And the Lord opened the eyes of the young man; and he saw: and, behold, the mountain was full of horses and chariots of fire round about Elisha."

The "horses and chariots of fire" were there

as really before the eyes of the young man were opened as afterward. The reason of his alarm was that he could not see them. His eyes were closed. It is even so still. The natural man is in darkness, and sees no light. He may look into the Bible, but in this state of mind he does not comprehend its meaning. It is a sealed book. It finds no response or welcome in his soul.

"Where, think you," inquires M'Masters, "did John Bunyan get his marvelous insight into the meaning of God's word? Not from learning, for he had little; not from his books, for he had few; but from his heart. It was full of eyes."

In like manner the natural man hears Christians describe their peace and joy, but he finds nothing answering to them in his own experience, and concludes that they must be untrue. He lacks spiritual discernment. He needs the touch of the divine hand upon his heart to open it to the perception and reception of the salvation which is in Christ Jesus. He needs a glimpse of the revealing light of faith, about which Charles Wesley wrote:

"To him that in thy name believes,
    Eternal life with thee is given;
Into himself he all receives,
    Pardon, and holiness, and heaven.

" The things unknown to feeble sense,
  Unseen by reason's glimmering ray,
With strong, commanding evidence,
  Their heavenly origin display.

" Faith lends its realizing light ;
  The clouds disperse, the shadows fly ;
The Invisible appears in sight,
  And God is seen by mortal eye."

This spiritual eye-sight needs further development in many of us who call Jesus our Master. It would make clear certain things which now seem strange, and perhaps impossible. Wonderful are some of the seasons of visitation from the presence of the Lord enjoyed by the true and holy. Better than the sight on the mountain top of the " horses and chariots of fire round about Elisha " are the spiritual glories which God's favored children have beheld in the very sunlight of his countenance.

" I well remember on one occasion," says William Carvosso, " while paying a visit to my Camborne friends, I was one night in bed, so filled, so overpowered with the glory of God, that, had there been a thousand suns shining at noonday, the brightness of that divine glory would have eclipsed the whole. I was constrained to shout aloud for joy. It was the overwhelming power of saving grace. Now it was that I again received the impress of the seal and the earnest of the Spirit in my heart. 'Beholding as in a glass the glory of the Lord,' I was 'changed into the same image from glory to glory,' 'by the Spirit of the Lord.' Language fails in giving but a faint description of what I then experienced. I can never forget it in time nor to all eternity. Many years before, perhaps not fewer than thirty, I was sealed by the Spirit in a somewhat similar manner. While walking one day between Mousehole and Newlyn I was drawn to turn aside from the public road, and, under the canopy of heaven, kneel down to prayer. I had not long been engaged with God before I was so visited from above, and overpowered by the divine glory, that my shouting could be heard at a distance. It was a weight of glory which I seemed incapable of bearing in the body, and therefore cried out, (perhaps unwisely,) 'Lord, stay thine hand.' In this glorious baptism these words came to my heart with indescribable power, 'I have sealed thee unto the day of redemption.'

"Giving glory to my God I can say to the present moment, I feel the blood of Jesus Christ cleanseth me from all sin. I am become a living temple, glorious all within. I can now love God with all my heart, with all my mind, and with all my strength. My inward heaven of joy and peace was, I think, never so great as of late. O Lord, help me to make some suitable return of love and gratitude! O stupendous redeeming grace! Feelingly can I sing this verse:

> "' O Love, thou bottomless abyss,
>   My sins are swallowed up in thee!
> Covered is my unrighteousness,
>   Nor spot of guilt remains on me,
> While Jesus' blood, through earth and skies,
> Mercy, free, boundless mercy, cries.' "

Rev. Edward Payson, when enjoying that remarkable manifestation of the Divine Presence which characterized his last days, during one of his conversations repeated this verse: "Thy sun shall no more go down; neither shall thy moon withdraw itself: for the Lord shall be thine everlasting light, and the days of thy mourning shall be ended." Turning to a young lady present he said, "Do you not think this is worth traveling over many high hills and difficult places to obtain? Give my love to my friends in Boston; tell them all I ever said in praise of God or religion falls infinitely below the truth." Again he said, "I seem to swim in a flood of glory which God pours down upon me. And I know, I *know*

3

that my happiness is but begun; I cannot doubt that it will last forever. And now is this all a delusion? Is it a delusion which can fill the soul to overflowing with joy under such circumstances? If so, it is surely a delusion better than any reality. But no, it is not a delusion; I feel that it is not. I do not merely know that I shall enjoy all this, I enjoy it now."

This is reality. This is bliss ineffable. It is the everlasting light of the Lord beaming upon the pathway of his child, like the silver light of an unclouded moon by night or the radiant glory of the sun by day.

"With bodily eyes, indeed," remarks a discerning writer, "no man ever has seen or ever can see God; but with the sight, the hearing, the sensibility, the capacity of a moral and immortal nature which has received Jehovah's image, he is apprehended. 'Mine eyes have seen the King Jehovah.' For that very purpose was the likeness to God originally imparted, for that is it now restored. That our first parents might know God, might commune with him, might talk to him, walk with him, dwell with him, enjoy the rapture of his presence and friendship, and prepare in this probationary life for an immortal fellowship with him, were they created and placed

in Eden. By the sufficient sacrifice, righteousness, and merit of the Son of God we regain the
lost image with all its privileges. Does not our
Lord distinctly teach that the very purpose of
our wondrous moral and immortal nature is to
know God both in time and eternity? 'This
is life eternal, that they might know thee the
only true God, and Jesus Christ, whom thou hast
sent.'

" Sin's debauchery of the soul's powers and character, with the subsequent persistent culture of unbelief, makes us to become oblivious of Deity; we
are as blind, obstinate, practical atheists. But the
faith-faculties of a God-given spirit-life, which
is in character like unto his own, introduce us
into his kingdom, into the realm of his presence
and glory, into the domain of his special person-
ality, his law, and his love. We behold him as
God, the Creator, the Source of life, the Ruler,
the Benefactor, the Father, the Redeemer, the
Guide, the Friend, the Comforter, the Helper—
the All and in All."

" None but the Spirit of God," says Spurgeon,
" can reveal God to any man, and the man himself
must receive a new and spiritual life before he
can know what the Spirit teaches." Who, then,
among the worldly-wise may dream of under-

standing God, when even the spiritual rather embrace him by love than grasp him by understanding? What is wanted is not an audible voice of God to confirm the evidences of our religion, but the touch and the voice of Christ to make us conscious within ourselves of the power of him to whom God bears witness. Not external but internal evidences are what we need. The best evidences in the world are what we call experimental, such as grow out of actual experience. It is a better thing for a man to live near to Christ, and to enjoy his presence, than it would be for him to be overshadowed with a bright cloud, and to hear the divine Father himself speaking out of it. The voice out of the cloud would but dismay and distract; the voice of Christ would cheer and comfort, and at the same time would be an equally powerful assurance to us of the divinity of the whole matter.

"Blessed are the pure in heart: for they shall see God." How can it be when Moses, hid in the cleft of the rock, could not see God's face and live? How can it be when Isaiah and Manoah said, "We shall die, for we have seen him face to face!" Yet here is the promise. It must be so. But how? Let Rev. Emory J. Haynes give his reply:

" Mozart and his friend, the royal huntsman, went forth arm in arm to the fields. The wind came up heavily through the copse of trees. 'Look!' says the hunter; 'it will startle a hare!' 'Listen!' says Mozart; 'what a diapason from God's great organ!' A lark rose on soaring wing, with its own sweet song. 'Look,' says the gamester; 'what a shot!' 'Ah,' says Mozart, 'what would I give could I catch that thrill!' There be dull souls who cannot see nor hear. Are they sick? 'O what misfortune!' Are they bereaved? 'Some enemy hath done this.' Are they well and prosperous? 'Good luck.' Not so. Pure heart. He can see God's hand in every sorrow chastening for good; God's face in every blessing; God's smile in the morning light, the blossoming harvest, and the evening shade. His heart is attuned.

"It has been done. What? You went from the church-yard to your closet; alone you bowed; you wept; you were crushed; you prayed; you closed your eyes; there came sweet peace, for you saw—Jesus."

It is this vision of the naturally invisible and this comprehension of the ordinarily incomprehensible which gives to the man of God his stability and unshaken fortitude. His faith stands

not in the wisdom of men, in what human
thought has devised and human skill perfected,
but in the power of God.   Mortal terrors cannot
intimidate him, for he is held above them by the
immortal presence.   Bodily temptations cannot
overthrow him, because he is sustained by the
power of an endless life.   Only when he lets go
of the high and holy things which God has revealed unto him by his Spirit has Satan power
to destroy him.   This explains why so many
humble, trusting hearts continue in the good old
way of the cross, notwithstanding the boasted
advancement of modern thought and the new-
fangled notions of popular æsthetics.   They are
out in deeper waters, and are borne by a stronger
tide than that which underlies the splash and
foam of current religious fashion.   For them the
Spirit is searching all things, yea, the deep things
of God.   They have not received the spirit of
this world, but the Spirit from above, and they
comprehend the good things so freely given by
the divine hand.   They compare not spiritual
things with natural, whether they are exactly
proportionate and pleasing, but spiritual things
with spiritual, and are chiefly concerned whether
they are making progress heavenward, and are
knowing more and more of the mind of the Lord.

Being spiritual, they judge all things, yet are themselves judged of no man. They are not weighed in earthly balances nor measured by worldly standards. Nevertheless, in all that goes to constitute true happiness and real use-fulness, they are as far advanced as their more superficial, and especially particular, fellow-pro-fessors.

The power of discerning spiritual things is a fruitful source of happiness. It strengthens a hundred-fold the arguments for the being of God, the truth of the Bible, and the divinity of our holy religion. The evidence which skeptics reject as insufficient Christians accept as entirely satisfactory, because, added thereto, are the ex-periences of their own hearts, the intuitions of their own souls. It follows, therefore, and is true to fact, that those who are most spiritual are least doubtful, or contrariwise, those who are most believing enter most largely into the com-forting experiences of a life hid with Christ in God.

The nature, reality, and sanctifying power of these spiritual revelations ought to be better un-derstood among us. When such is the case, when the truth that the Holy Ghost does make these persuasive inward impressions upon devout souls shall be fully apprehended, when it shall have that place in the visions of faith which it always has occupied in the Gospel system, "all serious doubts respecting the practicability of living above the power of sin will be put to flight." This is the belief of one who was in a position to pass intelligent judgment. His words are so di rectly to the point that this chapter may fittingly close with them:

"We have never met with a difficulty or ob- jection alleged against the doctrine of holiness which was not distinctly traceable to blindness, either speculative or practical, with regard to the revelations of Christ made to the soul by the Spirit. Some seem to have entirely dropped this vital truth out of their theology, while a much larger number appear to have had no experi- mental knowledge of its glorious import and transforming efficacy, and hence, while they hold it in theory, make it mean almost nothing. Many have this view of these revelations of Christ, that they are, when made at all, so mo- mentary and transient, that they can produce no permanent effect.

"An eminent clergyman in the city of Bos- ton avowed to a brother who was preaching the doctrine of holiness in that city, that he sometimes had momentary glimpses of Christ, in the light of which it seemed to him perfectly practicable to live without sin; but in a second thick clouds swept over and shut out the vision.

" This illustrates the idea which many have of these divine revelations or manifestations of Christ to the soul, namely, that they are altogether too transient and unfrequent to be relied upon in overcoming the world, the flesh, and the devil.

" But why are they thought to be transient? Because they are in fact so to some who, like the minister referred to, expect no more, and would esteem it fanaticism to look for long-continued and oft-repeated manifestations.

" If when the soul has a glimpse of Christ, it would consider that only a harbinger of coming light, and wait and expect and seek and cry aloud after the full revelations of Christ, it would soon realize the power of the Gospel. One of this character, a devoted minister, lately deceased, could testify that for years Jesus Christ had glowed down upon his soul with a light and glory, in comparison with which the light of the sun at noon was dim. These hasty glimpses, bright as they are, yet are as much

inferior to the radiance which Christ is ready
to pour continuously upon the soul, as a sudden gleam of light, darting through the rifted
clouds, is inferior to the blaze of the meridian
sun."

IX.

HOLINESS.

WITHOUT entering into any doctrinal niceties on the subject of the higher life, and without opening any of the old controversies which have been fruitful of so many ill effects, let a few points be stated in the way of making the subject clear.

And first of all, we have no dispute with any body as to the degree of holiness possible to man. This may safely be left with the Bible itself, and with every studious mind and enlightened conscience. We desire only to point out the fact that the Scriptures designate a blessing to which justified Christians had not yet attained. Call it what you will, refer to it as a state, a life, or only a phase of experience, it is there, and to its enjoyment professors of religion are invited.

Paul writes to the Thessalonians, "And the very God of peace sanctify you wholly; and I pray God your whole spirit and soul and body be preserved blameless unto the coming of our Lord Jesus Christ." 1 Thess. v, 23. That these Christians had already been justified appears from the account of their state of grace found in the first chapter of the epistle. That they had not attained the full blessing in store for them appears from the apostle's prayer.

Again, Paul exhorts the Corinthian Christians, "Having therefore these promises, dearly beloved, let us cleanse ourselves from all filthiness of the flesh and spirit, perfecting holiness in the fear of God." They were believers, then, being "dearly beloved" brethren. They had therefore been justified, yet they needed complete cleansing.

David acknowledged his transgressions and sin, and after praying that they might be blotted out, washed thoroughly away, he then besought the Lord to create within him a clean heart. Plenary pardon, observes Joseph Sutcliffe, was only half his request. He solicited purity, and purity without a stain. It is a small glory for a man to boast that his body and his character are free from gross sins, while his mind secretly feasts on impurity. We must pray that sin may not mere·ly be cropped, but wholly eradicated, and the whole man, body, soul, and spirit, "preserved blameless unto the coming of our Lord Jesus Christ." The indwelling of the Holy Spirit, and the constant application of the Redeemer's merits to keep us clean, are the surest preservatives from future sins.

Yet errors of thought and life will arise. Mistakes in judgment will lead to mistakes in practice, even in the most holy person, so that what is commonly known as "complete deliverance from sin" is deliverance only from wrong in motive or intent, and is entirely subject to weaknesses, infirmities, and mistakes.

"In the realm of our personal nature," says Rev. Dr. Asbury Lowrey, "sanctification does much, but not in the way of eradication. Its office is twofold. First, to expunge sin from every motion and impulse of the whole army of unreasoning propensities; second, to regulate, restrain, refine, and exalt all impulsive instincts. It does not extirpate or cripple a single constituent faculty. Nor does it blunt the sensibilities nor extinguish legitimate desire. The work of holiness in the empire of natural appetites and passions is to subjugate all to the absolute dominion of grace and keep all within the sphere of lawful indulgence."

Here we wish to introduce the testimony of Bishop E. S. Janes. It is not in any way pretentious or boastful, it makes use of no high-sounding phrases, but runs along so quietly and clearly, showing how his great soul was kept from sin, and was clean in the sight of God, that it may be regarded as a model of its kind.

"I want to say," he declares, "that I am saved from sin through Jesus Christ; that I have an increasing nearness to God and a more intimate fellowship with him, a greater sense of his gracious presence with me continually, by day and by night. If I have a title to any thing it is in heaven; if I have a hold on any thing it is on heaven. I know my probation is drawing to its close. I have had great opportunities to serve my Lord and Master, and to do good service for him. I have a very solemn account to render. I appreciate it more and more, and yet, through God's great mercy in Jesus Christ, I meet it without fear, for I believe that all my imperfections of service and devotion are forgiven for Christ's sake, and that he is the Lord, my Righteousness, and that through his mercy I shall give up my account with joy, and enter into the presence and beatitude of God. Blessed be his name! I awoke this morning with the hymn running through my mind which has in it this expression: 'Rivers of delight.' The thought never arrested my attention before. 'Rivers of delight!' What an expression! Celestial delight — rivers that never dry! 'Who shall make them to drink of

the river of thy pleasure, O Lord.' The pleasure
of God—a river of God's pleasure. I awoke this
morning with this passage in my mind : ' He
brought me to his banqueting house, and his
banner over me was love.' God's banquet —
spiritual food. You have been sitting at this
table of spiritual luxuries, of heavenly dainties, a
long time. It is a royal banquet; none but God
could furnish it. ' His banner over me was love.'
Not an ensign of authority, not an emblem of
power, but a banner of love. Who but Jesus
ever invited men to a standard he had stained
with his life-blood ? ' I, if I be lifted up, will
draw all men unto me.' The cross is his ensign.
Following this banner, we shall find our latest foe
under our feet at last."

Nor is any state of enjoyment or efficiency attained this side of heaven, if indeed ever, beyond
which growth and ascendency are no longer possible. No one has expressed this thought in better language than Canon Liddon.

" The spirit or soul of man," he says, " knows
itself to be capable, I will not say of unlimited,
but of continuous progress and development.
However vigorous the tree or the animal may be,
it soon reaches the point when it can grow no
more. The time comes when the tree has borne

all the leaves and fruit and buds which it can bear, when its vital force is exhausted, and it is no more. The animal may have done its best, it may have reached a high condition of strength and beauty, but when its limit is reached it can grow no more. With the soul of man as a living and thinking power it is far otherwise; he has never exhausted himself. When the man of science has made some noble discovery, when the literary man has written a great book, when the statesman has carried a series of important measures, we cannot say that he has exhausted himself. The spiritual man is indeed dependent on the material man, and as the body moves on toward decay and dissolution it extends something of the influence of its weakness and incapacity to its spiritual companion; but even then the soul resists this and asserts its separate existence; the mind of man knows that each separate effort, instead of exhausting his powers, tends to strengthen them, and so he will go on continually making larger and nobler and more vigorous efforts. So, too, is it with conscience and duty; with these there is no finality. One great act suggests another, one sacrifice makes another easier; the virtuous impulse in the soul is not like the growth in the tree, a self-exhausting force, but it is always moving on, always advancing. 'Be not weary in well-doing'—this is the language of the Eternal to the human will; but never is, 'Be not weary of growing' said to the tree or the animal, because organic matter differs from spirit in this, that it does reach the limit of its activity, and then it turns backward toward non-existence."

With this view the experience of Mrs. Elizabeth Prentiss coincides.

"I believe," she says, "in growth in grace, but I also believe in, because I have experienced it, and find my experience in the word of God, a work of the Spirit subsequent to conversion, (not necessary in all cases, perhaps, but in all cases where Christian life begins and continues feebly,) which puts the soul into new conditions of growth."

Here we have the suggestion that the soul only fairly begins its expansion when the light and love of God are poured out in full measure into its cleansed recesses, giving new vigor and freshness to its consecrated powers.

There is a constant reason for being holy in this life.

"Man," says Dr. Emmons, "is endowed with rational and moral powers which render him capable of holy exercises. He knows the difference
9

between holy and unholy exercises, and feels his moral obligation to exercise benevolent and pure affections toward all beings with whom he is concerned. This knowledge of duty lays him under obligation to do it. The obligation never ceases, and so he is constantly bound to fulfill it."

The divine law enjoins holiness. It says to every one, "Thou shalt love the Lord thy God with all thy heart, and with all thy soul, and with all thy mind, and with all thy strength; and thy neighbor as thyself." This law, which is founded in the nature of things, never has been, and never can be, abrogated. It binds Christians at all times, and requires them constantly to exercise holy affections. It carries their duty as high as it can be carried, and as high as the duty of angels or the saints in light. They can do no more than love God with all their heart, and their fellow-creatures as themselves. The Gospel, as well as the law, requires holiness. A multitude of precepts, prohibitions, and admonitions might be cited in proof.

1. Those which require saints to do every thing from love to God.

Paul, speaking to the saints in Corinth, says, "Whether therefore ye eat, or drink, or whatsoever ye do, do all to the glory of God." Again he says to them, "Let all things be done with charity;" that is, with pure, holy love. And to the Colossians he says, "Above all these things put on charity, which is the bond of perfectness. And whatsoever ye do in word or deed, do all in the name of the Lord Jesus, giving thanks to God and the Father by him." And again he says, "Whatsoever ye do, do it heartily, as unto the Lord, and not unto men." These divine precepts are universal and unlimited.

2. Those which enjoin a spirit of worship and activity.

Christians are required to "rejoice in the Lord always;" to "rejoice evermore;" to "pray without ceasing;" and to be "steadfast, unmoveable, always abounding in the work of the Lord." To his Christian brethren in Galatia Paul says, "If we live in the Spirit, let us also walk in the Spirit."

Peter, in his first epistle to Christians in general, says, "Wherefore gird up the loins of your mind, be sober and hope to the end for the grace that is to be brought unto you at the revelation of Jesus Christ; as obedient children, not fashioning yourselves according to the former lusts in your ignorance: but as he who hath called you is holy, so be ye holy in all manner of conversation; because it is written, Be ye holy, for I am holy." These precepts are exceedingly broad, and extend to every branch of a Christian's duty.

3. Those which insist that the devil and all his evil suggestions shall be resisted.

James says, "Resist the devil, and he will flee from you." Peter says, "Be sober, be vigilant; because your adversary the devil, as a roaring lion, walketh about, seeking whom he may devour: whom resist steadfast in the faith." "Wherefore," saith the apostle, "take unto you the whole armor of God, that ye may be able to withstand in the evil day, and having done all, to stand."

John says to them, "Love not the world, neither the things of the world. If any man love the world, the love of the Father is not in him." Paul tells them, "Be not conformed to this world; but be ye transformed by the renewing of your minds." And again he says, "Abstain from all appearance of evil."

Christians are urged also to feel and act with benevolence and propriety toward enemies. Christ commands them to love their enemies, and bless those who curse them, and to do good to those that hate them. The apostle gives a similar exhortation: "Bless, and curse not." "Be not overcome of evil, but overcome evil with good."

4. Those which urge believers to put away, mortify, and subdue all sin.

"The grace of God," says the apostle, "that bringeth salvation hath appeared to all men, teaching us that denying ungodliness and worldly lusts, we should live soberly, righteously, and godly, in this present world." And Peter says, ' Wherefore laying aside all malice, and all guile, and hypocrisies, and envies, and all evil speakings, as new born babes, desire the sincere milk of the word, that ye may grow thereby."

Paul says, "Abhor that which is evil; cleave to that which is good." Again he says, "Let not sin reign in your mortal body, that ye should obey it in the lusts thereof." And again he exhorts the Ephesians to "put off concerning the former conversation the old man, which is corrupt according to the deceitful lusts;" and to "put on the new man, which after God is created in righteousness and true holiness."

A persuasive plea for holy living might be grounded upon the teachings and practice of the whole Christian Church immediately subsequent to apostolic times. None who carefully read the writings of the primitive fathers can doubt that this theme was prominent among them, received, as it no doubt was, from the hearts and lips of the apostles themselves. The number of such writers is limited, but their testimony is explicit.

Clement, to whom Paul is supposed to refer in Phil. iv, 3, in his letters makes use of such expressions as these: "Of Job it is written, That he was just and without blame, true; one that served God and abstained from all evil." "They who have been made perfect in love, have, by the grace of God, attained a place among the righteous." He exhorts Christians to pray that they may be thus perfect, that so "they may live in charity; being unblamable, without human propensities, without respect of persons." To the Corinthians he says, "Ye were sincere, and without offense toward each other."

Barnabas, who, if not Paul's companion, was one of the same name living in the apostolic age, in the address to his epistle says to his readers, "I gave diligence to write in a few words, that together with your faith your knowledge might be perfect." Again, "But how does he dwell in us? The word of his faith, the calling of his promise, the wisdom of his righteous judgments, the commands of his doctrine: he himself prophesies within us, he himself dwelleth in us, and openeth to us who were in bondage of death the gate of our temple; that is, the mouth of wisdom, having given repentance unto us; and by this means has brought us to be an incorruptible temple."

Ignatius, a disciple of the apostles, having been, it is said, in the year 67, constituted by the apostle John, pastor of the Church at Antioch, over which he presided upward of forty years, and then sealed his testimony to the truth by a martyr's death, writing to the Church at Ephesus, gives utterance to the following beautiful words, the import of which cannot be mistaken: " Being followers of God, and stirring up yourselves by the blood of Christ, ye have perfectly accomplished the work that was connatural to you." " They that are of the flesh cannot do the works of the Spirit, neither they that are of the Spirit the works of the flesh. As he that has faith cannot be an infidel; nor he that is an infidel have faith. But even those things that ye do according to the flesh are spiritual; forasmuch as ye do all things in Jesus Christ." " Ye are, therefore, with all your companions in the same journey, full of God; his spiritual temples, full of Christ, full of holiness; adorned in all things with the commands of Christ. In whom also I rejoice that I have been thought worthy by this present epistle to converse, and joy together with you; that with respect to the other life, ye love nothing but God only." "That so no herb of the devil may be found in you; but ye remain in all holiness and sobriety both of body and spirit in Christ Jesus." "Of all which nothing is hid from you, if ye have perfect faith and charity in Christ Jesus, which are the beginning and end of life." "No man professing a true faith sinneth; neither does he who has charity hate any."

In his epistle to another Church he observes, "For inasmuch as ye are perfect yourselves, ye ought to think those things that are perfect. For when ye are desirous to do well, God is ready to enable you thereunto."

Polycarp, the disciple of John, in his epistle to the Christians at Philippi, uses this language: "Into which, (the epistle of Paul,) if you look, you will be able to edify yourselves in the faith that has been delivered unto you, which is the mother of us all; being followed with hope, and led on by a general love, both toward God and toward Christ and toward our neighbor. For if any man has these things he has fulfilled the law of righteousness; for he that has charity is far from all sin."

Chrysostom, "the golden-mouthed" bishop of Constantinople, who flourished in the fourth century, in his writings shows that the same spirit in respect to this doctrine which characterized the writings of the earlier fathers continued to flow right along in the Church. In his explanation of Gal. ii, 20, "I am crucified with Christ," etc., he says, "By saying Christ liveth in me, he means nothing is done by me which Christ disapproves; for as by death he signifies not what is commonly understood, but a death to sin; so by life he signifies a delivery from sin. For a man cannot live to God otherwise than by dying to sin; and as Christ suffered a bodily death, so does Paul a death to sin."

Athanasius, who flourished a half century earlier than Chrysostom, of wide celebrity, a pillar in the Church, in whose memory a famous creed was named, declared that "the Son of God, made man for us, and having abolished death, and having liberated our race from the servitude of corruption, hath, besides his other gifts, granted to us to have upon earth an image of the sanctity of angels, namely, virginity." "Nowhere, truly, except among Christians, is this holy and heavenly profession fully borne out or perfected; so that we may appeal to this very fact as a convincing proof that it is among us that true religion is to be found."

Of course Athanasius transcended the requirements of the law in attributing to Christians "upon earth an image of the sanctity of angels," but the passage shows how strong a hold upon his convictions the doctrine of holiness had.

About the beginning of the fifth century Pelagius was cited before a synod of fourteen bishops, charged with heresy in several things, and among the rest for saying unqualifiedly that "a man may be without sin if he will." Here is his explanation, in the correctness of which the entire synod concurred: "I have, indeed, said that man may be without sin, and keep God's commands, if he will. For this ability God has given him. But I have not said that any one can be found from infancy to old age who has never sinned; but, being converted from sin, by his own labor and God's grace, he can be without sin; still he is not by this immutable for the future."

Augustine, the great opposer of Pelagius, grounded his intense opposition upon the dogma, attributed to Pelagius, that "men either can be or are perfectly holy without the grace of Christ." "If I also allow," he says, "that some have been or are without sin, still I maintain that in no other way are they or have they been able to be so but by being justified by the grace of God, through Jesus Christ our Lord, who was crucified."

Augustine, in the heat of the controversy, afterward modified this view, and became an opposer of the doctrine in any form. Others shared his sentiments, and during the succeeding centuries, especially through the Dark Ages, and down to the Reformation under Luther, there were found men who opposed this doctrine of the Church. Luther gave it no direct aid, and it therefore regained not its prominence in the Church until Wesley revived it, stripped it of heretical attachments, and handed it down, explained and enforced, as the fairest heritage of spiritual Christianity.

As surely as there is any purpose at all in our existence on earth, and any divinity in the religion we profess to enjoy, so surely ought we to make the best use of our time, our powers, and our privileges in attaining unto this state of richest experience and highest efficiency. God has not given us more years, more strength, or more means of grace than are necessary, when best utilized, to train and fit our characters for the exalted stations they are to occupy in the eter-

nal world. "Kings and priests unto God!"
What wisdom and purity do the very words
imply!

But our station on earth is by no means con-
temptible. We are even now the children of a
King, and the heirs of promise. Privileges are
ours in the life of faith nobler and better than
worldly potentates are favored with. "There
are regions of bliss that may be reached by every
Christian. There are lands of Beulah where the
air is very sweet and pleasant, and the sun is always shining, and the birds are ever singing.
There are high mountains apart, where, dwelling
with Jesus, we are already in heaven." And we
believe it too. No matter how negligently we
may have lived, we believe there is an attainable
state of devotion high and holy and beautiful.
No doubt, at the door of entrance to our Church,
no matter what its name, we vowed to attain to
clean and sanctified lives.

President Charles G. Finney, in his day, earnestly contended for this truth. "Every evangelical denomination," he observed, "requires its
members to make a solemn covenant with God
and with the Church, in the presence of God and
angels, and with their hands upon the emblems
of the broken body and shed blood of the blessed

Jesus, 'to abstain from all ungodliness and every worldly lust, to live soberly and righteously in this present world.' Now if the doctrine of the attainability of entire sanctification in this life is not true, what profane mockery is this covenant! It is a covenant to live in a state of entire sanctification, made under the most solemn circumstances, enforced by the most awful sanctions, and insisted upon by the minister of God standing at the altar. Now what right has any man on earth to require less than this ?

"And again, what right has any man on earth to require this, unless it is a practical thing ?

"Suppose when this covenant was proposed to a convert about to unite with the Church, he should take it to his closet, and spread it before the Lord, and inquire whether it was right for him to make such a covenant, and whether the grace of the Gospel can enable him to fulfill it. Do you suppose the Lord Jesus would reply, that if he made that covenant, he certainly would, and must, as a matter of course, live in the habitual violation of it as long as he lives, and that his grace was not sufficient to enable him to keep it ? Would he in such a case have any right to take upon himself this covenant ? No, no more than he would have a right to lie.

"It has long been maintained by orthodox divines that a person is not a Christian who does not aim at living without sin; that unless he aim at perfection, he manifestly consents to live in sin, and is therefore certainly impenitent. It has been, and I think truly, said, that if a man does not in the fixed purpose of his heart aim at total abstinence from sin, and at being wholly conformed to the will of God, he is not yet regenerated, and does not so much as mean to cease from abusing God."

Other very thoughtful writers, who cannot be suspected of fanaticism on this subject, have given expression to sentiments entirely in accord with the foregoing.

Rev. Dr. Theodore L. Cuyler, notwithstanding the "no little crude nonsense" which he thinks has been said and sung about the "higher life," goes on to affirm that "the word of God does describe such a life, and it is the only sort of Christianity that the apostles preached and practiced. Jonathan Edwards got a fresh installment of it when he said, 'From that time I began to have a new idea of Christ, and of the work of redemption.' Such a higher life in the hearts of all our Church members would be a revival that would echo in heaven, and put a new face on our Christianity, and introduce a new and tremendous power for the conversion of a dead world to God."

Even Horace Bushnell thought it "curious to observe, when we read the Scripture, what an apparatus of cleansing God appears to have set in array for the purification of souls; sprinklings, washings, baptisms of water, baptisms of fire; fierce meltings also as of silver in the refiner's crucible; purifyings of the flesh and purgings of the conscience; lustrations of blood, even of Christ's own blood; washings of the Word, and washings of regeneration by the Holy Ghost;" and he declares it possible for the work of purification in this present life to go on until it cleanses "the very currents of thought, as it is propagated in the mind when the will does not interfere, and the mind is allowed, for an hour, to run its own way, without hinderance, one thing suggesting another, as in reverie, there may yet be no evil, wicked, or foul suggestion thrust into it. Or in the state of sleep, where the will never interferes, but the thoughts rush on by a law of their own, the mixed causes of corruption may be so cleared away, and the soul restored to such simplicity and pureness, that the dreams will be only dreams of love and beauty; peaceful and clear and happy, somewhat as we may imagine the waking thoughts of angels to be. There have been Christians who have testified to this heavenly sereneness of thought out of their own experience. And precisely this is what Paul refers to when he speaks of bringing into captivity every thought to the obedience of Christ. When the mixed causes are taken captive in the soul, and Christ is the law of the whole action, then, in the same degree, simplicity and purity return."

"A holy life," says Dr. Bonar, "is made up of a number of small things: little words, not eloquent speeches or sermons; little deeds, not miracles or battles; nor one great heroic act of mighty martyrdom, make up the true Christian life. The little, constant sunbeam, not the lightning; the waters of Siloam 'that go softly' in the meek mission of refreshment, not the 'waters of the river, great and many,' rushing down in noisy torrents, are the true symbols of a holy life. The avoidance of little evils, little sins, little inconsistencies, little weaknesses, little follies, indiscretions, and imprudences, little foibles, little indulgences of the flesh; the avoidance of such little things as those goes far to make up, at least, the negative beauty of a holy life."

And the positive side is equally distinct and clear.

Bates has compared the life of a saint to the labor of bees, who fly the livelong day either from their hives to the flowers, or from the flowers to their hives; and all their art and exercise are where there is fragrance or sweetness. So the holy soul ascends to God in sweet thought and ardent desire, and God descends into the soul by the communication of grace and comfort. The soul thus becomes a heaven enlightened with the beams of the Sun of righteousness, a paradise planted with immortal fruits, the graces of the sanctifying Spirit; and God walks with it communicating the sense of his love.

Not that there are no conflicts and crosses, sorrows and self-denials. These are inevitably a part of life on earth. But they have a brighter view.

"Sorrowful?" yes, "but always rejoicing." "Tribulation?" yes, "but in me ye shall have peace." And Paul speaks of "glorying in tribulation." "A fight of faith?" "yes, but always resulting in "victory," in "overcoming our foes."

When David was praying for the "clean heart," he included also the petition, "Restore unto me the joys of thy salvation."

10

The Saviour speaks of his disciples having "fullness of joy;" his joy, his peace. Paul speaks of "rejoicing evermore," of the "peace of God which passeth all understanding, keeping the heart and mind through Christ Jesus." And Peter tells us of a "joy that is unspeakable and full of glory."

All the developments of spiritual life are not alike easy of attainment. There are what Spurgeon denominates "the common frames and feelings of repentance and faith and joy and hope which are enjoyed by the entire family; but there is an upper realm of rapture, of communion, and conscious union with Christ, which is far from being the common dwelling-place of believers. All believers see Christ, but all believers do not put their fingers into the prints of the nails, nor thrust their hand into his side. We have not all the high privilege of John to lean upon Jesus' bosom, nor of Paul, to be caught up into the third heaven. In the ark of salvation we find a lower, second, and third story; all are in the ark, but all are not in the same story. Most Christians, as to the river of experience, are only up to the ankles; some others have waded till the stream is up to the knees; a few find it breast-high, and but a few—O how few!—find it a river to swim in, the bottom of which they cannot touch."

Many never make the effort to get out into deep water. They are afraid to venture. They lack faith in the almighty Hand that buoys up every actively trusting soul. They see the breakers of doubt and temptation and difficulty, and they keep on the shoreward side. They have heard of others who ventured through and found the calm, smooth, deep waters of love, but they do not follow. They prefer the wrestlings and tossings inevitably belonging to a shallow experience, praying ever,

> " When rising floods my soul o'erflow,
> When sinks my heart in waves of woe,
> Jesus, thy timely aid impart,
> And raise my head, and cheer my heart."

They go no farther. They could if they would. They might pray,

> " Now let me gain perfection's height;
>   Now let me into nothing fall,
> As less than nothing in thy sight,
>   And feel that Christ is all in all.

> " To real holiness restored,
>   O let me gain my Saviour's mind;
> And in the knowledge of my Lord,
>   Fullness of life eternal find.

"O'erwhelmed with thy stupendous grace,
I shall not in thy presence move;
But breathe unutterable praise,
And rapturous awe, and silent love."

In respect to a life of holiness, believers are something like voyagers on the deep. When a man embarks on an ocean steamer it is his privilege to secure any kind of passage—first-class, second, or third. He may occupy a first-cabin berth, be a steerage passenger, or even have his place in the hold. So in regard to the higher and lower stories of the ark of salvation. The price is paid for us. "Jesus paid it all; all the debt I owe." There is abundance of room wherever we choose our lot. Welcome awaits us in the highest place. Indeed, that is where God would have us be. He invites us all to the upper room. "The Spirit and the bride say, Come." He shows no partiality. "Whosoever will" is the merciful and comprehensive word. Brother, choose your berth.

Evidently there is more interest in this subject than might at first be inferred from a glance at the Church and society. Those who have taken upon themselves the vows of the Christian life are conscious that, having a name to live, they are also entitled to all the benefits and blessings of a life hid with Christ in God; in other words, that it is folly to profess religion and not enjoy the full measure of its power. Nominal religion in substance amounts to nothing. It is not worth the profession. It gives no satisfaction to its subject and commands no respect from the world. Few professors of religion, who are not for a purpose hypocrites at heart, are contented with lip and life service only; they want the satisfying portion—the real, comforting, and soul-thrilling power, which only the fully saved enjoy. Some, because of this yearning of the soul, this going-out after God, this longing after the fullness of life which is in Christ, are constrained to open their bosoms to others; they counsel with those whom they believe to have attained, and are already perfect ; they are open and earnest seekers after the blessing of entire sanctification, and when at last they enter into this rest, they are known, perhaps, as professors of the blessing of perfect love. But many nominal Christians do not venture an open acknowledgment of their secret yearnings. They hesitate to refer to it, fearing that, in the present state of society, they will be regarded as weak or peculiar, or that a committal of themselves to a line of special seeking may be found in their way under some other of the varying circumstances of life. But nearly all, who have in any degree tasted and seen that the Lord is good, hunger and thirst after righteousness, secretly and unscripturally, it may be, yet consciously, and in the better moments, earnestly. It would doubtless astonish many ministers who seldom allude to this subject, either in the pulpit or in pastoral work, to find a majority of Church members alive to it, and when once drawn out, very tender of soul, and ready immediately to be directed into the experience of purity. No amount of disputation or alleged fanaticism can hide from intelligent Christian minds the plain Bible truth that Jesus came to save to the uttermost, and that it is a blessed privilege, as well as solemn duty, to be cleansed "from all filthiness of the flesh and spirit, perfecting holiness in the fear of God."

And is there any thing in religion more attractive than this? Certainly to love God with all our hearts, and our neighbor as ourselves; to have the image of God stamped on our souls, the life of God manifest in our mortal flesh, the mind that was in Christ clearly perceptible in all our expressions and ways; walking as Christ also walked; "endeavoring to keep the unity of the Spirit in the bond of peace;" returning not railing for railing, but disarming criticism by circumspect lives; constantly laboring, praying without ceasing, rejoicing evermore, and in every thing giving thanks; there is in such undeniable characteristics of personal holiness something very charming and beautiful.

To fully appreciate this "we must realize the ugliness of sin; for sinfulness is the only alternative to holiness. If a man is not holy in heart and life he is sinful in heart and life; and sin is the most hideously ugly thing in the universe. All the gilding and attractions with which Satan and wicked men seek to invest it cannot make it beautiful. It is deformity, imperfection, impurity, defilement—terms used to designate essential ugliness. By contrast with these qualities of sin, we may see the intrinsic beauty of holiness. It is purity, symmetry, perfection, likeness to God, who is the sum of all perfection. Sin is hell in the soul, insubordination, anarchy of all its passions and powers, which are not only in conflict with conscience, but are in conflict with one another; insomuch that 'the wicked are like the troubled sea when it cannot rest, whose waters cast up mire and dirt. There is no peace saith my God to the wicked.' Holiness is peace, and heaven in the soul, the harmony of all its powers

with one another, with conscience, and with God.
The sinful soul is a cage of unclean birds, a
whited sepulcher, if its possessor is outwardly
circumspect, but within full of rottenness and
dead men's bones. The holy soul is the abode
of all pure thoughts, affections, desires, purposes; the abode of the immaculate Trinity.
'We will come unto him, and make our abode
with him.'"

How little does it matter whether the power of
the Spirit, resulting in such living, overshadows
the believing soul in an instant, as no doubt is
often the case, so that from that time he enjoys
inward and outward holiness, to which he was
before an utter stranger, or whether it comes in
the gradual unfolding of a long consecrated life!
The main point is that the soul is truly transformed, that there is no deception, no delusion,
but a deep and constant communion with the
Father and the Son, whereby the whole heart is
surrendered and the whole life governed and con-
trolled by the purest principles of the divine
word.

The truth is, no one experience, or class of experiences, as to this doctrine, can ever become a
universal standard. Here, as in conversion, and
in intellectual exercises, every man in his own

order. Controversies as to the method of becoming holy may wage until the millennium, and nothing be settled. Nevertheless souls may continue to trust God for full salvation, and testify to the experience of it, supporting the testimony by holy living and dying. In this, not in the long-drawn arguments of theorists, the beauty of holiness appears. To this earnest-minded believers would better give attention. In the contemplation of it there is profit, and in the experience of it there is spiritual and eternal gain. To have the inward man of the heart renewed after the image of God, cannot but strike every eye that God hath quickened — every enlightened understanding.

"The ornament of a meek, humble, loving spirit will at least excite the approbation of all who are capable, in any degree, of discerning spiritual good and evil. From the hour men begin to emerge out of the darkness which covers the giddy, unthinking world, they cannot but perceive how desirable a thing it is to be thus transformed into the likeness of him that created us."

God is love. This is the image of him we most readily acquire. Love is of God, and by loving we show that we are in God.

This love or charity is the "bond of perfectness." It gives value to all other graces. Without it faith, that could remove mountains and understand all mysteries, is of no profit. Without it man is dead while he liveth, and viewed from the stand-point of eternity, all his works are valueless. Meditation, prayer, consecration, are all essential in advancing to a state of holiness, but they must abound in charity—the love of God for himself, and man for the love of God.

Some one asked the Bishop of Geneva what he must do to attain perfection.

"You must love God with all your heart, and your neighbor as yourself," was the reply.

"I did not ask wherein perfection lies," was the rejoinder, "but how to attain to it."

"Charity," said the Bishop again, "is both means and end, the only way by which we can reach that perfection, which is, in truth, after all, but charity itself. St. Paul says, 'I will show you a more excellent way;' and then he enlarges more fully upon charity. It is the life of all that is good; without it all graces die: it is the only way to God; the only life of the soul, for it brings us forth from the death of sin into the life of grace: it kindles faith and hope. Just as the soul is the life of the body, so charity is the life of the soul."

"I know all that," said the inquirer, "but I want to know how one is to love God with all the heart, and his neighbor as himself?"

"The best way, the shortest and easiest way of loving God with all one's heart," the Bishop replied, "is to love him wholly and heartily. There are many besides you who want me to tell them of methods and systems and secret ways of becoming perfect, and I can only tell them that the sole secret is a hearty love of God, and the only way of attaining that love is by loving. You learn to speak by speaking, to study by studying, to work by working; and just so you learn to love God and man by loving. If you want to love God perfectly, go on loving him more and more; never look back, press forward continually. When you are making most progress you will most constantly press on, never believing yourself to have reached the end; for charity should go on increasing till we draw our last breath."

Again, he added, "If we really love God, we shall strive to promote his glory; we shall gladly render him every service he requires; we shall be jealous for our neighbor's welfare, and seek to promote it as our own, because this is acceptable to God. This is true charity, real solid love of

God for his own sake, and of man for God's sake."

In the processes of sanctification the Holy Ghost, the third person of the ever-blessed Trinity, is a very active agent. Religious writers are all agreed in this.

"Turn with me for a moment," says the late Dr. Henry Cowles, the eminent educator and commentator of the Congregationalist Church, "to a short but precious chapter in the history of true religion. We have it in the Acts of the Apostles. It is the history of the men who were baptized with the Holy Ghost. It will be remembered that at the time of their baptism they were already Christians of a certain sort—that they had followed Christ with more or less of devotion for some three years or more, and had apparently left all for his sake. Still they had many crude notions, great unbelief, and not a little fear of man. They were sanctified very partially. A mighty work remained to be wrought in their hearts. There is room for a change more striking than even that of their first conversion, and the Spirit of God can effect it. The Spirit comes. His sweet and mighty effusions are shed forth on them all. And what are they now? Their hearts are filled with love—

yes, filled, absolutely filled, with love. The historian tells us often that they are of one accord, of one heart, and of one soul. See, too, what love they bear to Christ. Mark how they rejoice to be counted worthy to suffer shame for his sake. See how, as on lightning's wing, they bear the story of his love to all nations. Note the love they manifest for a dying world. It would seem as if love had become their ruling passion; and in some of its manifestations toward their Saviour, each other, lost sinners, or their enemies, it were bursting forth in mighty, ceaseless currents.

"And where now is their former love of the world? What do they care henceforth for its favors or its frowns? What for its honors? O they have laid them down with all joy at their Saviour's feet, and have taken up his cross for their crown of glory.

"And how marvelously, too, have their fears vanished away. Where is he, that one among them who, a few days ago, quailed before a servant-maid, and, through fear of ill-treatment, forsook his Master, and absolutely took his oath that he did not know him? Yes, where is he? He is brought before that very council which struck such terror through his soul but yesterday. Summoning all the dignity and majesty of a Jewish

Sanhedrin, they fiercely interrogate him, to know by what power he is acting. And does he quail now? No. The historian tells us that Peter, 'filled with the Holy Ghost,' made his defense fearlessly, preached to them the Gospel of Jesus boldly, confounded them utterly, and finally left them with this resistless appeal to their consciences: 'Whether it be right in the sight of God to hearken unto you more than unto God, judge ye. For we cannot but speak the things which we have seen and heard.' Acts iv, 19, 20. Such is one feature of the change wrought in a soul 'filled with the Holy Ghost.'"

A few passages of Scripture will make plain the fact and nature of the Spirit's work:

"God hath from the beginning chosen you to salvation through sanctification of the Spirit and belief of the truth." "But we all, with open face beholding as in a glass the glory of the Lord, are changed into the same image from glory to glory, even as by the Spirit of the Lord."

Peter says to believers, "Ye have purified yourselves, by obeying the truth, through the Spirit." Christ is that truth which the Spirit presents to our minds, yielding to which we experience purity. The Spirit never speaks of himself; he glorifies Christ. He never acts independently of Christ. He takes of the things of Christ and shows them unto us. He brings the Godhead into our souls. The love of God shed abroad in our hearts is "by the Holy Ghost, which is given unto us." The Father and the Son come and make their abode with us because "we are built together for an habitation of God through the Spirit." The Spirit leads us into all truth. He dwells with us, and is in us. We are sealed with the Holy Spirit of promise. He is given us as a Teacher and Comforter. How much, then, ought we to know and enjoy. The Spirit is bestowed upon us to give us "the light of the knowledge of the glory of God in the face of Jesus Christ," that we may enjoy the fullness of Christ's redemption.

Of his own experience under this gracious baptism Dr. Cowles, in his work on "Holiness of Christians," says, "In the sorrows and the joys of the Christian life it has been my lot to participate somewhat deeply. Spontaneously do I seize the language of another and subscribe myself, 'your brother and companion in tribulation, and in the kingdom and patience of Jesus Christ.' Permit me, therefore, to unbosom myself to you so far at least as to detail briefly what God has wrought for me. This I do, not because I wish to make myself prominent—for nothing is more revolting to my soul—but mainly for two reasons: 1. That from the deepest dust I may testify to the great goodness and kindness of God toward me; and, 2. That I may bear my testimony to the practical value of the blessed truths which I have been urging you to study, embrace, and obey.

"It is now about twenty years since I have supposed myself to be a child of God; and during most of this period I have had little or no doubt of my being accepted of him through the merits of his Son. Yet there has been a sad deficiency in the practical power of the Gospel upon my heart to subdue sin, and keep me under the protecting wing and inspiring eye of my Saviour. I have been conscious of sins, and have struggled against some of them long and hard, and almost in vain. For many years my intellectual perceptions of truth were always in advance of my moral sensibilities in view of it. Over this I have mourned bitterly as a grievous sin, and often have thought that my inveterate habits in this respect were incurable.

"But I did not apprehend the adequate fullness of the provisions of the Gospel. I was resisting sin more by dint of resolutions than by the aid of simple faith in Christ. I had not seen that there is grace enough provided to justify the rational expectation of being delivered in this life from all known sin, and from all sin as fast as revealed to us by God's word and Spirit. With these views, how could I expect more victory over sin, and more ample communications of the Spirit than I had?

"Through a most kind providence my mind, more than a year since, was strongly turned to the investigation of this subject, especially as taught in the Bible. The result on my spiritual state remains to be briefly told.

"1. My views of the provisions of the Gospel have been greatly enlarged, and have become more definite. The Bible taught me to regard them as entirely adequate for their object—the supply of all my spiritual wants. 2. I see with great clearness how certainly and intensely the heart of Christ is set upon sanctifying his Church, and how ardently the energies of each person in the Trinity are devoted to this work. 3. Consequently I have learned to ask for greater blessings. No spiritual blessing for myself seems too great to be sought of God in prayer. I have a precious conviction—worth more than both the Indies—that I cannot please God better than in

11

asking every moment to have my capacities absolutely filled with spiritual gifts and graces. I know that the more earnestly and confidingly I pray to be just like Jesus Christ, the more acceptable will my prayer be, and the more sure of being answered. 4. Of course I have learned to expect greater blessings. And, 5. Of course also I have received greater blessings. God has shown me that my moral insensibilities under intellectual apprehensions of truth can pass away in a moment under the melting touch of the Spirit's power. On Gospel truths and promises my soul now feasts with a luxury which none can ever know but by experience. Every thing about religion becomes a blessed reality. I know not how in better and fewer words to describe my state. Religious truths are transformed into solid realities. The shadowy objects of a dim and weak faith have assumed the full form and vivid features of real existence."

Mrs. Mary C. Nind, a well known Christian worker, has given to the press an interesting narration of her entrance into full spiritual light. She was born near London, England; converted at the age of five years, became a Sunday-school teacher at twelve, and united with the Congregationalist Church at fourteen. Coming to America, she continued in active service for the Master. Her religious studies and associations naturally led her to wonder whether she might not have a richer experience than she had hitherto enjoyed; whether, indeed, there was not perfect rest of soul in store for the believing heart.

"Must I go on," she reasoned, "thirty, forty, fifty, sixty years, and still have to fight against my easily besetting sins, and every now and then be conquered? Is there no hope of victory all the time? Cannot Jesus, the physician of soul and body, heal my soul as quickly and as perfectly as he healed the sick while on earth, saying to the leper, 'I will; be thou clean. And immediately his leprosy was cleansed?' Thus I reasoned and soliloquized, then went to a good old deacon for a solution, and told him all, and he answered me, 'Mary, you want too much; you must expect to fight and struggle and to be overcome by sin and Satan sometimes through your life, but ere you die, before you go to heaven, Jesus will take all your sins away, and make you holy.' My heart was heavy as I turned away, not believing the theology given, and feeling an earnest desire to die suddenly, and soon, if I must go on battling for threescore years and ten. But I lived on, passed through childhood, early womanhood, into the relations of wife and mother, growing in grace, still at work for Jesus, having a good amount of joy in the Lord, and yet, as thousands do, sinning and repenting, gaining a victory, then losing a battle, struggling, fasting, resolving, praying, hoping, longing to be free. For nearly forty years I was 'in the wilderness,' so near the goodly Canaan, and yet not entering in, for I had no Joshua to tell me 'I was well able to go up and possess the land,' nor did I know how to enter.

"'But God, who is rich in mercy,' having seen my tears, heard my sighs, sobs, and prayers—saw me beating against my cage, trying to be free. He sent a man of God from the Theological Seminary in Chicago, who preached the doctrine of the 'Higher Life,' and he enjoyed the experience he preached. I listened eagerly. I longed for Sunday to come that I might know more. How clear and well-defined the way—the narrow way —how much consecration included and involved. How the light of the Spirit did shine upon the truth. How the Lord did discover to me that there was much to be surrendered—love of applause and honor, some worldly ambitions, love of dress, desire to be rich, and many other things. After some conflicts, sharp and strong, I resolved to be and do all the Lord would have me be and do, cost what it would. I laid aside my jewelry after hearing an excellent sermon upon the text, 'Let your women adorn themselves in modest apparel,' and as on my knees I told the Lord I did it for his sake, the blessed baptism fell on me as the seal of the divine approval. This little act cost me some bitter opposition, but I steadily adhered, and rejoiced in my freedom. God's word was studied from cover to cover to learn his will. With earnest prayer I sought to know the mind of the Spirit. Meetings were attended, conversation with the pastor, the reading of books which would throw light upon the doctrine and experience, and after many, many months, I came to the conviction: 'The Bible teaches we may "be holy," we may "be cleansed," we may have "rest" even here, we may be "sanctified wholly," we may be "saved to the uttermost."' Judgment, intellect, conscience, say yes to it all, but inbred sin yet remained.

" Anew I consecrated myself to the Lord and his service, and with new consecration came new joy. Two years and eight months passed on, the Lord all the while setting his seal to the steps I had taken. The children all converted, and many of my Sunday-school scholars; the consecration, so far as I had light, complete, but the blessing of a clean heart not obtained. . . .

"In the year 1867, at Winona, Minn., I was led by a dear sister, a busy mother like myself, to trust the Lord for salvation from inbred sin, the cleansing of my heart, which should bring to me what I had so long desired—'the rest of faith.' In my own room on Thursday evening, just before going to prayer-meeting, the work was done, and the baptism of melting love and the gentle hush of tenderness and rest of soul was mine. And I said, again and again, 'Can it be, after all these years of weary waiting and hard struggling, that I have rest?' I went to prayer-meeting and tried to tell it, but it was the rest unspeakable. All night long I was too happy to speak, and a hundred times or more I said, 'Blessed Jesus, I have rest, sweet rest. Emptied of self, filled with God, Mary C. Nind has rest. Halleluiah!' The morning came, the best morning of my life, then, the power of God had prostrated my body— physically weak, but O such rest!—my face, my voice, my step, my bearing was changed; my children noticed it. I told them I had rest. I cannot say it has been from that time until now unbroken rest, but I can say that through grace it has been the habit of my soul, and whenever I have lost it, I have by faith pursued till I re-gained it. I cannot live or work successfully for Jesus without it. It cost me much to seek it and find it—too much to ever lose it. It has been to me 'the pearl of great price.' These years since I have been in this valley of blessing have been years of 'Beulah land,' years of rest, victory, peace, joy, and glad-continued service; and as I go I sing,

> "'O come to this valley of blessing so sweet,
> Where Jesus will fullness bestow;
> O believe and receive and confess him,
> That all his salvation may know.'"

Many other testimonies might be incorporated here, but they would swell this volume to too large proportions. One more must suffice.

"I need an angel's power," was the acknowledgment of Rev. D. Osborn, "to express the heaven of sweetness and love which flows into my soul, and the fullness I see in Christ Jesus my Lord. I know that my present Redeemer from all unrighteousness lives, and lives now for me. But I can no more tell the depth and breadth of perfect love than a man could tell the measure of the mighty mass of waters if he were thrown overboard in the middle of the Atlantic.

'God is love:' I know it, I feel it; 'and he that dwelleth in love, dwelleth in God, and God in him.' O what a measureless ocean! A child of earth submerged in the deep sea of God's pure love!

"I now see a fullness and a meaning in the blessed Bible, which before I could not discover. I read before with pleasure, but now I can read and comprehend in the light of the experience of the blessed doctrine of holiness. When I read that perfect love casteth out fear, I understand it. I know what it is to have the fear of sufferings, of death, and of the burning judgment, cast out by perfect love. And yet how small and insignificant am I. I seem to sink into nothing, while Christ is all in all.

"I think I know what Payson means when he says, 'The Sun of righteousness has been gradually drawing nearer and nearer, appearing larger and brighter as he approached, and now he fills the whole hemisphere, pouring forth a flood of glory, in which I seem to float, like an insect in the beams of the sun.' I think I have enjoyed something of this great blessing before, but only a taste. I never before saw its mighty fullness; and that fullness I hold only by simple faith, moment by moment; while all I am lies on the altar as an entire sacrifice to God, trusting him for all that is to come, who has said, 'My grace is sufficient for thee.'

"To all who seek this great blessing I would say, With all on the altar, expect it by simple faith, just now; and to those who do enjoy it, I would say, With all on the altar, hold it by simple faith, just now. May God multiply the living witnesses of perfect love!"

How many there are who feel that sin, in some of its forms, has dominion over them, and they long for complete deliverance. Yet they have no clear conception of the way of escape. They have, perhaps, heard of the doctrine of holiness, or have given it just enough attention to imagine that it is some modern contrivance, some man-made theory, used by agitators to call attention to themselves or keep up a religious stir. They know not that full salvation is only the common salvation rightly improved and enjoyed. Their eyes are not opened to the truth that right before them in their neglected Bibles are the very promises and assurances upon which this whole doctrine rests. They might turn to the Old Testament and hear the Divine voice proclaiming through Ezekiel:

"Then will I sprinkle clean water upon you,

and ye shall be clean: from all your filthiness, and from all your idols, will I cleanse you. A new heart also will I give you: and a new spirit will I put within you: and I will take away the stony heart out of your flesh, and I will give you a heart of flesh. And I will put my Spirit within you, and cause you to walk in my statutes, and ye shall keep my judgments, and do them."

Or to the New Testament, and hear Paul say:

"The Lord make you to increase and abound in love one toward another, and toward all men, even as we do toward you: to the end he may stablish your hearts unblamable in holiness before God."

Upon these and kindred passages they might rest their weary souls. They are all made to us, and by them we may become partakers of the divine nature, and thus escape the corruption that is in the world through lust. It is a sad truth that "we have not yet begun to appreciate the fullness, depth, and richness of the provisions of the Gospel." We appreciate the value of money, the joy of social life, the pleasures of time and sense, but not the value of the true riches, the joy of a holy life, and the exalted and pure pleasures of saving and sanctifying grace.

A few there are, indeed, who have partaken of a measure of the fullness, a taste of this blessedness, but such live a separate, even a lonely, life, and are counted a peculiar people. Nearly all the Churches believe in holiness as a theory under some name, but the pulpits of the day, echo not with the preaching of it. Here and there a pastor preaches an occasional sermon on the necessity of a holy life, but the intervals between are so extended that the doctrine is soon lost sight of. What should be a standard theme in regular pulpits is rarely discussed at all.

Alas, that it is so! We cannot neglect this experience and be guiltless. We cannot neglect it and be happy. We cannot neglect it and be useful to the extent of our responsibility. Holiness gives power to the Church and the ministry, and neither education, nor wealth, nor numbers, can compensate for its absence.

Holiness is by faith. The whole Christian life is a life of faith. " Believe on the Lord Jesus Christ and thou shalt be saved " is a condition which applies from the first token of penitence to the highest point of spiritual attainment.

Frances Ridley Havergal, that scholarly English woman of such rare religious insight and training, wrote a hymn that tells the whole story.

Her own grace and earnestness are couched in its expressive lines:

> "Church of God, beloved and chosen,
>   Church of Christ for whom he died,
> Claim thy gifts and praise the Giver!
>   'Ye are washed and sanctified.'
> Sanctified by God the Father,
>   And by Jesus Christ his Son,
> And by God the Holy Spirit,
>   Holy, holy, three in One.
>
> " By his will he sanctifieth,
>   By the Spirit's power within,
> By the loving hand that chasteneth,
>   Fruits of righteousness to win;
> By his trnth and by his promise,
>   By the word his gift unpriced,
> By his own blood, and by union,
>   With the risen life of Christ.
>
> "Holiness by faith in Jesus,
>   Not by effort of thine own,—
> Sin's dominion crushed and broken
>   By the power of grace alone,—
> God's own holiness within thee,
>   His own beauty on thy brow,—
> This shall be thy pilgrim brightness,
>   This thy blessed portion now.
>
> " He will sanctify thee wholly;
>   Body, spirit, soul, shall be,
> Blameless till thy Saviour's coming
>   In his glorious majesty;

He hath perfected forever
  Those whom he hath sanctified;
Spotless, glorious, and holy,
  Is the Church, his chosen Bride."

But this faith will hardly be exercised by those who have not engaged in the preparatory work of a complete consecration. As a means of attaining to a clean heart, a sanctified life, the real disposition on our part to rise so high, to gain so much, ought to be appropriately manifested.

"Are you willing," inquires Bishop Foster, in his 'Heritage of Faith,' "to devote all, entirely, forever, to the Lord? Holiness implies this; if we are not willing to make the consecration, we are not willing, and hence not ready, to receive holiness."

Guarding, as we think, wisely against the illusion, "Believe that you are sanctified and you are," he says:

"It is meet, when we have consecrated our all as well as we can, that we should trust in God; not in our act, but in God; not that he has sanctified, because we have consecrated ourselves, but that he will accept the consecration, and both sanctify and send us the witness. Until the witness comes we will not say that we are entirely sanctified—we will not even believe we are; we will look to be, and wait in expectation until we are, and then we will rest in God—ay, will rest while we wait — in the faith that it shall be done."

Such an attitude is becoming to the Christian. It shows him as hungering and thirsting after righteousness in the blessed certainty of being filled. It proves the genuineness of his conversion, inasmuch as having tasted and seen that the Lord is good, he would tarry at the feast for complete satisfaction. It answers to the sentiment of St. Paul, who made it the "one thing" of his spiritual endeavor to forget the things behind and reach forth unto those before, ever pressing toward the mark for the prize. Let us, therefore, as many as be perfect, be thus minded. Even whereto we have already attained, let us walk by the same rule, let us mind the same thing.

X.

IN POWER—THE MINISTRY.

LET us consider some of the qualifications necessary to higher success in the ministry of today. Success is what we want; success in saving souls.

And, first of all, ministers must be adapted to their calling. They must have natural ability for its arduous work. They must be men of God, bold, strong, devoted, sanctified; recognized by all as being men among men; and loving their labors more than they love their lives.

They must be students. They must have college training if they can get it. Colleges do not make brains, but they improve what a man has. Experienced non-graduates in the ministry regret, when alone with their English Bibles, their libraries, and their God, that they have not the advantages of collegiate discipline. They know that greater usefulness might be theirs if prepared to grapple directly and promptly with the problems which educated skeptics and worldlings (though these classes are not all educated) are

continually thrusting upon public attention. It is
not the business of the Gospel minister, primarily,
to confute infidelity, but it is his business to be
ready to give to every man that asketh a reason
for the hope that is in him, with meekness and
fear.

All talk about self-education is practically an
argument for the schools. Every self-educated
minister is a standing proof that ministers need
education, else why do they study to acquire it?
And it would not be difficult to prove that the
long and necessarily defective efforts at self-train-
ing are not the best. Our conclusion is, if a man
would be most useful in the ministry, let him first
know that God wills he should preach; then let
him use the gift that is in him, adding to it by all
possible diligence, in the colleges, if possible, or
in connection with them as a necessary alternative; if neither is possible to him, still let him
study every-where, in all ways and times, that by
some means he may prove himself a workman
needing not to be ashamed of his intellectual, any
more than of his spiritual, acquirements. The
matter is important. The fathers are falling, and
there is danger that the sons will be less rigor-
ous in their voluntary efforts at self-mastery.
The conditions have all changed. Satan's allies

bear polished weapons of keenest edge. How shall Israel's captains cope with them? Do you say, with sling and stone, as David did? But David used the best weapon of his time, and, having done his part, God took care of the rest. But these are days of needle-guns and Winchester rifles, and a commander would be little better than an idiot who would send his soldiers to battle with primitive weapons, as against the destructive appliances of modern art. Man has his province, and in it he is to act wisely. God can and must be trusted to-day the same as of old, but he will not do for man what man can do for himself. It is a major part of every minister's duties to qualify himself for the most effective service in fighting the Lord's battles.

A good theological training is especially needful in the modern preacher. Fundmental doctrines are too seldom preached, and not given their rightful proportions in relation to each other.

A preacher who has not himself the right perspectives of truth, who holds doctrines in a confused and distorted order, and misplaces them relatively, giving to some erroneous projections, and keeping others too far in the back-ground, however orthodox he may be, is liable to mislead his people, and produce all the practical evils of a

12

false teaching. If theology were a misshapen mass of independent truths, the responsibilities of the public teacher would be far less than they now are. The only way in which he could in that case mislead would be by the complete omission of some vital doctrines, and the substitution of erroneous ones. But theology is a system of related truths, and it is the business of the preacher to understand these relations, and properly adjust them in his public ministrations. If he make the subordinate the prominent, error is just about as effectually preached as if he omitted the fundamental doctrines altogether. "As a man thinketh so is he." Teach him to think that a non-essential is an essential, or that a vital doctrine is of little consequence, and straightway the error crops out in his conversation and life. Let a minister imbibe false notions of duty and responsibility, and teach them to his fellows, and the result is disastrous to the spirituality of the Church.

Earnestness is an essential element in the ministry.

A writer made a great stir recently by publishing an article on the insincerity of the modern pulpit. What ever of error crept into his sayings, it is yet deplorable that even a liberalist should find occasion to impeach the pulpit at so vital a point. Whatever else preaching is, it ought to be sincere; and it would seem that if preachers had truth fixed in their own minds in its relative proportions, and in its bearings on duty and destiny, there would never be even a semblance of insincerity in appeals to dying men.

We would most respectfully and urgently entreat the ministerial brother, whose eyes may follow these lines, to examine his own heart and head and life and writings, whether he has not trifled with the sacred office by giving undue prominence to some personal whim, some beautiful but unimportant idea which was calculated to please the fancy, but not to bless the soul, some point of doctrine so small as to require a year's searching among the great words of inspiration to find a single one to confirm it, and then only by torture. Does it not appear as if Paul had been thus examining himself when he declared with such earnestness to the brethren at Corinth, "I am determined to know nothing among you save Jesus Christ, and him crucified?" If ministers felt for souls as they ought; if they believed in the doctrine of hell, as they profess; if they were really of one work, as they have vowed; would there not be warnings and entreatings with tears, such as the world too seldom witnesses, and such as would rouse sleeping mortals from their delusive dreams? Without attempting to clear members of the Church from one iota of their responsibility in this matter, we can but believe that if the eighty thousand ministers of this country could have their hearts burn within them as if on fire of the Holy Ghost, and their lips touched as with a live coal from the holy altar, this nation would speedily witness such a Pentecost as has not been known since the time when the cloven tongues crowned the brows of the consecrated disciples who went out to turn the world upside down.

"To preach well," says a writer, "ministers must live well.

"When a man delineates religion not so much as the result of study and reasoning as a matter of his own history; when he unfolds it with that inexpressible character of life and earnestness which accompany truth drawn from one's own bosom, he cannot be powerless. There is nothing vague and uncertain, nothing obscure or unintelligible in the speech of such a one. He presses earnestly toward his object. His heart's desire is that his hearers may be saved. The power of that inward emotion he cannot conceal. Chains cannot bind it. It thaws through the most icy habits. It bursts from the lip. It speaks from the eye. It

modulates the tone. It pervades the whole manner. It possesses and controls the whole man.
He is seen to be in earnest; he convinces; he
persuades.

"It is a most important service which religion
has rendered, not only to the eloquence of the
pulpit, but to every department of Christian literature, by putting the *faculties under the pressure and power of a grand motive.* The heart of
man must be pressed and well nigh crushed before it will give out its wine and its oil. Woe
is me, said Paul, if I preach not the Gospel of
Christ. He who would preach with force and
effect must subject himself to that religious sense
of responsibility which is alone competent to
bring into action every dormant faculty; and
bear about him the solemn and weighty reflection
that he watches for souls as one that must give
account. Whenever the heart and conscience
exert their combined power in this direction,
every talent will be employed; the whole man is
urged to full and efficient action. Cast such a
man into prison, and, like Bunyan, 'ingenious
dreamer,' will he describe the progress of the
soul to God; confine him to a bed of sickness, and,
like Baxter, will he sweetly muse and write of the
'rest' of saints in heaven; blind his eyes in total

night, and 'celestial light' will shine inward, enabling him, like the glorious Milton, to

> 'See and tell
> Of things invisible to mortal sight.'

Fetter him with chains, and in the very presence of kings and governors, he will, like Paul, reason about a judgment to come; nail him to the cross, his heart will still palpitate with inextinguishable love, and his latest breath will be spent, like his Master's, in praying and speaking for others' good."

Devotion to work is an essential of success in all callings, especially in the Gospel ministry. Selfishness here is a fatal defect. There must be a spirit of self-forgetfulness and self-sacrifice, a willingness to live unknown to fame, and to be forgotten after death by the worldly historian. The true minister must be ready to exclaim, with the apostle, "Yea, doubtless, and I count all things but loss for the excellency of the knowledge of Christ Jesus my Lord." "He knows that fame is but a breath, variable as the wind, and honor a mere condition that may change into dishonor in the next revolution of public opinion or change of the circumstances about him. Even the earth upon whose surface the scenes of honor and in-

famy are played interchangeably in the great
drama of life will be consumed by spontaneous
combustion, and lie a 'smoking clinker on the
grates of eternity.' Deeper concerns than 'the
bubble reputation' interest the man of God. He
is in earnest to save himself, and the divine commission to save others burns in his soul like fire
shut up in his bones; he, therefore, has no disposition to toy with the frothy honors and evanes-
cent joys of earth. 'Who wants amusement in
the flame of battle? 'Twere treason to the soul
immortal, her foes in arms, eternity the prize.'"*

To be successful, ministers must be men of one
work. The Church demands that pastors do
faithfully what is contemplated in their ordina-
tion vows. Secular enterprises and private spec-
ulations never yet made a minister more respected
by his membership. They may admire his genius,
and even follow after him in his personal pursuits,
but his spiritual counsels will lose their power,
and his religious labors be attended with a dim-
inution of success. The apostles knew whereof
they wrote when they declared, "It is not reason
that we should leave the word of God and serve
tables." The whole order of the Church, its
trusteeship, stewardship, and general officiary,

* Rev. J. D. Barbee.

is based upon a recognition of the principle that the ministry is for the preaching of the word, and for that only, whether in the form of public discourse, or of personal appeal in the midst of pastoral service.

Direct personal appeal is the one successful method of soul-winning to-day. The time is past when general exhortation alone will suffice to turn sinners to righteousness. The great evangelists organize their forces for personal work. The great pastors make personal work the burden of their ministry. Rev. Dr. J. O. Peck, of New Haven, who, at the end of twenty-five years as a regular pastor, had been instrumental in leading over four thousand souls to Christ, early learned the secret of highest ministerial usefulness, namely, "personal private labor with individuals." Private persuasion of individuals is the secret of any success in winning men to God. In the sweeping revivals of these latter days, hundreds are converted at home, or in little inquiry circles, before they come to the public meetings. Pastors must know their sheep, and if they would get any valuable accessions to their flocks, they must go out and seek them individually from among the lost. They must make this work the one business of their lives. They "have nothing

to do but to save souls." For this they are consecrated and ordained. Failure here cannot be
compensated for by success elsewhere. Through
sweeping revival, or steady spiritual growth,
every pastor should cease not to labor night
and day with tears until salvation comes to his
people. Sweet in eternal worlds will be the rest
of such a worker. Rev Charles D. Bell, D.D.,
once drew the following full-length portrait of a
faithful pastor. It portrays his spirit rather than
his success, but the success of such a man can
hardly be portrayed:

> A man he was who, from his earliest youth,
> Had sought and found the hidden heart of truth,
> Whose law found just expression in his mouth.
>
> His was a noble mind, pure, docile, calm,
> His lips for wounded souls kept healing balm,
> Prayers for the sad, for happy ones a psalm.
>
> His gaze was on the unattained, the far,
> Which shone before him like the Polar star;
> For things unseen, he scorned the things that are.
>
> His face caught beauty from the soul within,
> His ear was deaf to earthly strife and din,
> His mind to that of angels was akin.
>
> He ever linked high thoughts to loving words,
> Which stirred to music all the spirit's chords,
> As stir the leaves the songs of forest birds.

The beautiful had in his heart a share—
The flowers, the birds, all things of earth and air—
He looked abroad and found God's creatures fair.

Life was to him no idle, empty dream,
No withered leaf caught by the whirling stream,
And borne where'er the current might beseem.

He filled each passing hour with earnest deeds,
In action lived while he professed in creeds,
And of high aspirations sowed the seeds.

His voice was raised for suff'ring souls and poor,
And he could pity where he could not cure;
When wronged himself, he knew how to endure.

His heart was as a sacred altar-fire,
On which burned faith and hope and pure desire,
But which of meaner passions was the pyre.

Although no halo gleamed around his head,
Yet o'er his life a saintliness was shed.
All saw to worldly pleasure he was dead.

So, as the narrow path he daily trod,
And walked the world, unspotted, with his God,
With sweetest praise and prayer he cheered the road.

All that he lost for Christ he counted gain,
And living not for earth, lived not in vain,
But sowed for future harvests the rich grain.

Wise as the serpent, harmless as the dove,
He dwelt on earth, but lived in heav'n above,
Child like and simple, full of faith and love.

Rev. Thomas Binney, of England, about forty
years ago, preached a wonderful sermon to minis-

ters from the text: "The pastors have become brutish, and have not sought the Lord, therefore they shall not prosper, and all their flocks shall be scattered." Jer. x, 21. The point Mr. Binney made was the importance of private prayer to those who sustain the sacred function; it was essential to ministerial success. If there is a hard and pitiable case in this world it is that of a spiritual guide in whom personal religion has declined, from whom religious success has departed, and nothing remains but professional propriety and functional formality. How surely in such a case does the flock scatter and decay by estrangement and division, the truly devout drawing off, and those remaining in the fold proving any thing but sheep. Surely such instances in these days are not attributable to any informality in inducting pastors to the sacred office, to any want in them of intellectual ability, nor, as a rule, to any heresy or immorality. The one defect which poisons every thing is that such pastors are not men of earnest, frequent private devotion. This is the hidden evil among us which is retarding our growth, giving Satan advantage over us, and bringing the Church of God into disrepute.

A minister once said to a man who was breaking stone on a turnpike, "I wish I could break the hearts of sinners like you break those stones." "You might," said the man, "if you were as much on your knees as I am."

The spiritual life must be nourished and sustained in a minister the same as in other men—he cannot live on his own official acts. The customary work of preachers, especially the numerous social engagements, are not promotive of ministerial piety. Our Lord, perhaps, had such drawbacks in view when he said to his disciples, on their return from a successful official tour, "Come ye apart into a desert place and rest awhile." How often did he himself repair to the mountain top or lonely retreat to pour out his heart in the fervor of prayer and devotion. His example in this regard has ever been too little followed by his under-shepherds.

The personal religious condition of a pastor necessarily modifies every thing he does. The perception of divine truth, and therefore the power to exhibit it with clearness and vividness, depend, by a law of nature, upon the culture and preservation of a state of mind in harmony with truth itself. Cold and superficial, indeed, will be the pulpit and altar efforts of that pastor whose fellowship is with the world more than with the

Father, whose communion is with himself and his fellow-men on secular themes more than with God in the wrestlings of secret prevailing prayer. The great ministers who have moved mankind heavenward and Godward have been men of habitual devotion.

We believe and teach that prayer, in addition to its reflex influence on the mind, is a direct means of obtaining divine help. If it is not, then, we are left without any way of securing divine guidance, and all the promises of Scripture are utterly without meaning. Our help cometh from the holy hill. Success is of the Master, not of the servant. If a minister have not God's aid in God's work he is left in a condition of appalling abandonment, acting and laboring alone in a vocation recognized by all mankind as the most solemn and responsible known to the earthly life. Think of a poor, solitary, unaided man trying to do a divine thing in a state of sinful and melancholy independence. No human being can involve himself in a sadder plight than to assume the functions of the Christian ministry, and live an indifferent, prayerless life. He stands between God and the people, not to convey but to obstruct divine influence, and hinder the progress of religious impression. If there is one woe deeper than another in the future world, he may expect to reap it who thus weighs his own selfish interests in the balance against immortal souls.

Perhaps the following striking remarks from the pen of Dr. Philip, in his good old "Life and Times of Whitefield," will be as new, forcible, and inspiring as any thing that can be said. Certainly there is no reason why ministers at the present day may not preach in "the demonstration of the Spirit and of power," as well as in ancient times. We are yet under the dispensation of the Spirit, and the condition of the Spirit's presence and help is the same as of old. Whose soul has not been pained and whose heart has not been sick in listening to the dull monotony—soulless and lifeless—of some who minister in the name of Christ.

What idea can those dear brethren have of the nature of the high commission which they bear, whose pulpit performances consist, to a great extent, of labored essays, learned, perhaps, and elegantly written, but savoring little of the apostle's theme, "Jesus Christ and him crucified," and delivered in a manner which indicates any thing else than a soul inspired and burning with the message of love? But to the extracts.

"It is high time that the Church of Christ

should consider, not only the duty of depending on the Spirit, but also the import and importance of the 'demonstration of the Spirit,' in preaching. That is more than the demonstration of orthodoxy. It is more than the demonstration of either sound scholarship or hard study. It is even more than the demonstration of mere sincerity and fidelity. Sincerity may be cold and fidelity harsh. Even zeal may be party rivalship or personal vanity, while it seems holy fire, searching only for incense for the glory of God and the Lamb. To preach in the 'demonstration of the Spirit' is even more than bringing out the 'mind of the Spirit' faithfully and fully. The real meaning of his oracles may be honestly given, and yet their true spirit neither caught nor conveyed. 'What the Spirit saith unto the churches' may be repeated to the churches without evasion or faltering; but it will not be heard as his counsel or consolation unless it is spoken with something of his own love and solemnity. He is the Spirit of power, and of grace, and of love, as well as the Spirit of truth, and of wisdom, and, therefore, he is but half copied in preaching if only his meaning is given. That meaning lies in his mind, not merely as truth, nor as law, nor as wisdom, but also as sympathy, solicitude, and love for the souls it is addressed unto. The words of the Spirit are spirit and life, and therefore the soul, as well as the substance of their meaning, is essential to faithful preaching. They can hardly be said to be the words of the Holy Ghost when they are uttered in a spiritless and lifeless mood.

"This will be more obvious by looking at the 'truth as it is in Jesus.' In him it is grace as well as truth. All his heart and soul and strength breathe and burn in his words. His motives are a part of his meaning. He explains the great salvation that he may endear and enforce its claims at the same time. He makes us feel that he feels more for our souls than words can express. He compels us to see a beaming in his eye, and to hear a beating of intense solicitude in his heart, and to recognize a fixedness of purpose in all his manner, unspeakably beyond all he says. The real pleading of the Saviour with sinners begins where his words end. His weeping silence, after speaking 'as never man spake,' tells more of his love to souls than all his gracious words. We feel that he feels that he has gained nothing by his preaching unless he has won souls. He leaves upon every mind the conviction that nothing can please him but the heart, and that nothing would please him so much as giving him the heart. No man ever rose or can rise from reading the entreaties of Christ without feeling that Christ is in earnest, is intent, is absorbed, to seek and save the lost.

" The apostles evidently marked this with great attention, and copied it with much success when they became 'embassadors for Christ' by the ministry of reconciliation. Then they did more than deliver the truth he taught. They tried to utter it with his solemnity, tenderness, and unction. They tried to put themselves in ' Christ's stead ' when Christ was no longer on earth to beseech men to become reconciled to God. This was the 'demonstration of the Spirit.' Saying what Christ did was not enough for them; they labored to say it as he did, or in the spirit and for the purpose he had preached the Gospel. Thus the truth was in them as it was ' in Jesus;' not merely as true, but also as impressive, persuasive, absorbing. They spoke the truth as he had done, ' in the love of it,' and with love to the souls it was able to make wise unto salvation.

" And this is not impossible even now, although apostolic inspiration be at an end. The best part of the Spirit's influences—love to the Gospel and immortal souls—is yet attainable, and as easily

13

attained as any other ministerial qualification. A
minister should be as much ashamed and more
afraid of being unbaptized with the Holy Ghost
and fire, as of being ignorant of the original
language of the Holy Scriptures. Men who can
demonstrate the problems of Euclid, or the import of Greek or Hebrew idioms, have no excuse
if they are unable to preach with the 'demonstration of the Spirit and of power.' The same attention to the latter demonstration which they gave
to the former would fill them with the Holy
Ghost, and fire them with holy zeal.

" The minister must be a holy temple unto the
Holy Ghost who would have the Spirit speak to
the hearts of man by him. Never does a preacher dupe himself or endanger others more than
when he imagines that the Spirit will give power
to the Gospel among his people, while it has not
power upon himself. God makes ministers a
blessing to others by blessing themselves first.
He works in them in order to work by them."

O for such consecrated and powerful men of
God! The sin-cursed and dying world needs
them. The too-listless and inactive Church requires them. We believe they will be raised up.
The tide will turn. The Almighty will not forsake his people. He will plead his cause. Truth

will triumph. Through human agency, in the pulpit and pew, and in the busy, bustling world, the power of the Highest will ere long be displayed in turning thoughtless and reckless humanity from the power of Satan unto God. Then shall spirituality prevail; then shall the beauty of holiness appear; then shall men see that on true piety the noblest humanity is built; then shall the world know that

> " Religion pure,
> Unchanged in spirit, though its forms and codes
> Wear myriad modes,
> Contains all creeds within its mighty span,
> The love of God displayed in love of man."

XI.

SPIRITUAL MAXIMS.

STIRRING SPIRITUAL MAXIMS CHOSEN FROM THE WRITINGS OF BISHOP JOSEPH HALL, THOMAS A KEMPIS, THOMAS ADAM, FENELON, MADAME GUYON, HANNAH MORE, DYER, PERE LA COMBE, MATTHEW HENRY, RICHARD BAXTER, JEAN PIERRE CAMUS, FRANCIS DE SALES, AND OTHERS.

" In God's own might
We gird us for the coming fight,
And, strong in him whose cause is ours
In conflict with unholy powers,
We grasp the weapons he has given,—
The Light and Truth and Love of Heaven."
—J. G. WHITTIER.

" Thy life's a warfare, thou a soldier art,
Satan's thy foeman, and a faithful heart
Thy two-edged weapon, patience thy shield,
Heaven is thy chieftain, and the world thy field."
—QUARLES.

"' Life is before ye !' from the fated road
Ye cannot turn ; then take ye up the load ;
Not yours to tread or leave the unknown way,
Ye must go o'er it, meet ye what ye may.
Gird up your souls within you to the deed,
Angels and fellow-spirits bid ye speed."
—MRS. BUTLER.

"Think not of rest; though dreams be sweet,
Start up, and ply your heavenward feet.
Is not God's oath upon your head,
Ne'er to sink back on slothful bed;
Never again your loins untie,
Nor let your torches waste and die,
Till, when the shadows thickest fall,
Ye hear your Master's midnight call?"—KEBLE.

If we pronounce condemnation upon ourselves, Christ is able to save; but if we excuse ourselves and impenitently await the condemnation of Christ, we are forever undone.

Never go to war in another man's armor. David was wiser than this. Saul put upon him a coat of mail, but he would not meet Goliath in it because he was untrained. Choosing a smooth stone from a brook, he put it in his oft-tried sling, and with it smote his giant foe to the death. Every man in his own order.

The cross of Christ produces two seemingly different effects in a believer: it makes him sensible of his own vileness, yet prompts him to work for the good of others.

Good works follow salvation just as naturally as saving faith precedes it. For this reason Paul felt perfectly safe in uttering the challenge, "Show me thy faith without thy works, and I will show thee my faith by my works." Faith is the blossom which brings forth the fruit of obedience.

The day is lost in which we gain no step toward heaven, and worse than wasted in which we lose ground.

Christ's free man, heaven-taught and Spirit-led, aims at perfection in the love of God, and grieves only for the want of it.

Most men depend upon to-morrow for happiness and achievement, yet they never overtake it; they ignore to-day which is ever present, until life becomes an eternal yesterday. Work while the day lasts.

Death does not change character, it only fixes it. Bring, then, to the hour of death such a character as you can be happy with to all eternity.

Sin known and pardoned is heaven on earth, and is the song of praise in glory; sin known and unpardoned is the source of misery here, and will be a burning torment hereafter.

FROM BISHOP JOSEPH HALL.

When we go about any enterprise of God it is good to see that our hearts be clear from any pollution of sin, and when we are thwarted in our hopes it is our best course to ransack ourselves, and to search for some sin, hid from us in our bosom, but open to the view of God.

There can be no mercy in injustice, and nothing but injustice in not fulfilling the charge of God. The death of malefactors, the condemnation of wicked men, seem harsh to us; but we must learn of God, that there is a punishing mercy. Cursed be that mercy that opposes the mercy of God. Let our own sins first fall.

With us there is no way to victory but fighting, and the strongest carries the spoil; God can give victory to the feet as well as to the hands; and when he will, makes weakness no disadvantage. What should we do but follow God through by-ways, and know that he will, in spite of nature, if we trust in his grace, lead us to our end.

It is not so much glory to God to take away wicked men as to overrule their evil to his own holy purposes. How soon could the Supreme Ruler of heaven and earth rid the world of bad members !

The great Commander of the world hath set every man in his station; to one he hath said, Stand thou in this tower and watch; to another, Make thou good these trenches; to a third, Dig thou in this mine. He that gives and knows our abilities can best set us to work.

Evil is uniform, and beginning at the senses takes the inmost fort of the soul, and then arms our own outward forces against us.

As Satan, so wicked men cannot abide to lose any of their community. If a convert comes home the angels welcome him with songs, the devils follow him with uproar and fury, his old partners with scorns and obloquy.

Who can complain either of solitariness or opposition that hath God with him; with him not only as a witness, but as a party? Even wicked men and devils cannot exclude God, not the bars of hell can shut him out. He is with them by force, but to judge and punish them; yea, God will be ever with them to their cost; but to protect, comfort, save, he is with none but his.

The only way to find comfort in an earthly thing is to surrender it into the hands of God.

Wickedness hath but a time; the punishment of wickedness is beyond all time.

No good man would be saved alone.

No good heart ever repents having done well.

Small and unlikely means prevail when God intends an effect.

It is holy and safe to be jealous of the first occasions of evil, either done or suffered.

The heart that is bent upon God knows how to

walk steadily and indifferently between the pleasures of sin and fears of evil.

The guilty conscience can never think itself safe.

It is the duty of men, much more of Christians, to advise against sin.

A small authority will serve for a loving admonition.

We love not the Church if we easily leave it.

God never graces the idle with his visions. When he finds us in our callings, we find him in the tokens of his mercy.

Frequency of meeting with God gives us freedom of access, and makes us pour out our hearts to him as fully and as fearlessly as to our friends.

God loves to over-deserve of men, and to exceed, not only their sins, but their very desires, in mercy. O what goodness is that he hath laid up for them that love him!

O Lord, thy hand is not shortened to give; let not ours be shortened or shut in receiving.

God will be waited on, and will answer quickly, but the consummation of his blessings he will give at his leisure.

God loves we should take pains for our spiritual food.

God delights to have us live in a continual dependence upon his providence, and each day renew the acts of our faith and thankfulness.

We shall find difficulties in all good enterprises; if we be sure we have begun them from God we may securely cast all events upon his providence, which knows how to dispose, and how to end them.

No Christian may think it enough to pray alone. He is no true Israelite who is not ready to lift up the weary hands of God's saints.

God hath said and done enough for us to make us trust him.

The God of mercy will not impute the slips of our infirmity to the prejudice of our faithfulness.

It is not possible a man should have any long conference with God, and be no whit affected.

We are strangers from God; it is no wonder if our faces be earthly ; but he that sets himself apart to God shall find a kind of majesty, and respect put upon him in the minds of others.

Christian modesty teaches a wise man not to expose himself to the fairest show, and to live at the utmost pitch of his strength.

Moses put a veil upon his face, but when he went to speak with God he pulled it off. Hypocrites are contrary to Moses; he showed his worst to men, his best to God; they show their best to men, their worst to God.

God, as he is himself eternal, so he loves permanency and constancy of grace in us: if we are but a flash and away, God regards us not.

God expects of us an improvement of the graces we have received.

It is presumption and sacrilege to bring profane coals to God's altar. We do this when we bring zeal without knowledge, misconceits of faith, carnal affections, the devices of our will-worship, and superstitious devotions. These flames were never of his kindling; he hates both altar, fire, priest, and sacrifice.

True faith is courageous, and makes nothing of those dangers wherewith others are quelled. There is none so valiant as the believer.

If God bear us in his arms when we are children, yet when we are well grown, he looks we should go on our own feet; it is enough that he upholds us, though he carry us not.

To hear of the loving-kindness of God is pleasant, but to behold and feel the evidences of his mercy is unspeakably delectable.

The main care of a good heart is still for the public, neither can it enjoy itself while the Church of God is distressed. As faith draws home generalities, so charity diffuses generalities from itself to all.

The way to obtain any benefit is to devote it, in our hearts, to the glory of that God of whom we ask it: by this means shall God both please his servant and honor himself; whereas, if the scope of our desires be carnal, we may be sure either to fail of our suit, or of a blessing.

FROM THOMAS À KEMPIS.

Let us endeavor to conquer ourselves, to daily wax stronger, and to grow in holiness.

If we would endeavor like brave men to stand in the battle, surely we should feel the assistance of God from heaven.

For he who giveth us occasion to fight, to the end we may get the victory, is ready to succor those that fight, and that trust in his grace.

If thou dost not overcome small and easy things, when wilt thou overcome harder things.

There is no order so holy nor place so secret as that there be not temptations or adversities in it.

Gird up thy loins like a man against the vile assaults of the devil; bridle thy riotous appetite, and thou shalt be the better able to keep under all the unruly motions of the flesh.

O how sweet and pleasant a thing it is to see brethren fervent and devout, well-mannered, and well-disciplined.

He that knoweth best how to suffer will best keep himself in peace; that man is conqueror of himself and lord of the world, the friend of Christ, and an heir of heaven.

A man must strive long and mightily within himself before he can learn fully to master himself, and to draw his whole heart unto God.

The devil sleepeth not, neither is the flesh as yet dead; therefore cease not to prepare thyself to the battle; for on thy right hand and on thy left are enemies who never rest.

Why fearest thou to take up the cross which leadeth thee to a kingdom?

In the cross is salvation, in the cross is life, in the cross is protection against our enemies, in the cross is infusion of heavenly sweetness, in the cross is strength of mind, in the cross joy of spirit, in the cross the height of virtue, in the cross the perfection of sanctity.

There is no salvation of the soul nor hope of everlasting life but in the cross.

Take up therefore thy cross and follow Jesus, and thou shalt go into life everlasting. He went before, bearing his cross, and died for thee on the cross; that thou mightest also bear thy cross, and be a partaker with him in glory.

Go where thou wilt, seek whatsoever thou wilt, thou shalt not find a higher way above nor a safer way below than the way of the holy cross.

The cross is always ready, and every-where waits for thee.

The more thou knowest, and the better thou understandest, the more strictly shalt thou be judged.

There is no peace in the heart of a carnal man, nor in him that is given to outward things, but in the spiritual and devout man.

Esteem not thyself for the height of thy stature, nor for the beauty of thy person, which may be disfigured and destroyed by a little sickness.

I have often heard that it is safer to hear and take counsel than to give it.

If we esteem our progress in religious life to consist only in some outward observances, our devotion will quickly be at an end.

The beginning of all evil temptations is inconstancy of mind and small confidence in God.

He that hath true and perfect charity seeketh himself in nothing, but only desireth in all things that the glory of God should be exalted.

Those things that a man cannot amend in himself or in others he ought to suffer patiently until God order them otherwise.

The life of a good, religious person ought to excel in all virtues, that he may inwardly be such as outwardly he seemeth to men.

Never be entirely idle; but either be reading, or writing, or praying, or meditating, or endeavoring something for the public good.

What canst thou see anywhere that can long continue under the sun?

Thou thinkest, perchance, to satisfy thyself, but thou canst never attain it.

Couldst thou see all things present before thine eyes, what were it but a vain sight?

Lift up thine eyes to God in the highest, and pray him to pardon thy sins and negligences.

Leave vain things to the vain, but be thou intent upon those things which God hath commanded thee.

Shut thy door upon thee, and call unto Jesus, thy beloved.

Stay with him in thy closet, for thou shalt not find so great peace anywhere else.

O my brother, cast not away thy confidence of making progress in godliness; there is yet time, the hour is not yet past.

Who shall remember thee when thou art dead? and who shall pray for thee?

Now, whilst thou hast time, keep unto thyself everlasting riches.

Think on nothing but the salvation of thy soul, care for nothing but the things of God.

Suppose that thou hadst up to this day lived always in honors and delights, what would it all avail thee if thou were doomed to die this instant?

When thou hast Christ thou art rich, and hast enough. He will be thy faithful and provident helper in all things, so that thou shalt not need to trust in men.

For men soon change, and quickly fail, but Christ remaineth forever, and standeth by us firmly unto the end.

A lover of Jesus and of the truth, and a true inward Christian, and one free from inordinate affections, can freely turn himself unto God, and lift himself above himself in spirit, and rest in full enjoyment.

By two wings a man is lifted up from things earthly, namely, by simplicity and purity.

Simplicity ought to be in our intention, purity in our affections. Simplicity doth tend toward God; purity doth apprehend and taste him.

If there be joy in the world, surely a man of a pure heart possesseth it.

And if there be anywhere tribulation and affliction, an evil conscience best knoweth it.

Blessed is the soul which heareth the Lord speaking within her, and receiveth from his mouth the word of consolation.

Blessed are the ears that gladly receive the pulses of the divine whisper, and give no heed to the many whisperings of this world.

Blessed are the eyes which are shut to outward things, but intent on things within.

Blessed are they that enter far into inward things, and endeavor to prepare themselves, more and more, by daily exercises, for the receiving of heavenly secrets.

Blessed are they who are glad to have time to spare for God, and who shake off all worldly hinderances.

Teach me, O Lord, to do thy will; teach me to live worthily and humbly in thy sight; for thou art my wisdom, thou dost truly know me, and didst know me before the world was made, and before I was born into the world. Let thy truth teach me, guard me, and preserve me safe to the end.

14

FROM THOMAS ADAM.

Christ says, "Take up the cross;" and very evident it is that some of his commands, literally taken, have the cross in them. Take this out, and then wherein does he differ from other legislators? or what remains but a bare religion of nature? which, we may be sure, will never bear too hard upon flesh and blood.

Christ in me will be the same God-devoted, sin-hating, soul-loving, self-denying, suffering, laboring Christ that he is in himself.

Faith gives me Christ, and love from faith gives me to my neighbor.

Lord, have mercy upon me, and help me; I am surrounded with enemies which I cannot resist but in thy strength, and must fall a prey to them without thy assistance. Suffer not thy name to be dishonored in the destruction of thy poor creature, and the triumphs of the powers of darkness over thy promise for my salvation. Let the confession of my weakness, and of my dependence upon thee, prevail with thee in Christ to stand up in my defense; and do thou get the victory, and be glorified in thyself, and in thy own goodness. Amen!

The will of God is my pole-star, and, with my

eye constantly upon it, I shall be carried safely through all storms and tempests.

If God gives internal comfort, it is not that we may live upon it, but to support and animate us to some further end.

To-day's duty is no discharge for to-morrow: every day has its own peremptory demand upon us, not only for repetition, but advancement. It is a saying of St. Basil, that the soul would starve, as well as the body, without a continual renewal of its proper food; and St. Paul's motto in the midst of such a course of labor and activity as would quite have sunk the spirits of another man was, FORWARD!

God made us for eternity, and his aim in all he does is to bring us happily to it. Hence the necessity of pain, sickness, crosses, work, and war, to break the strong chain which binds us to the world, and force us to take part with God in his grand design.

We have time enough to prepare for eternity, and should be thankful that we have none to spare.

Nature says, If I may not sin, let me die; grace says, Let me die rather than sin.

On earth, prayer, improvement, waiting; in heaven, praise, perfection, happiness.

Get a step toward heaven, endeavor to master some evil temper, and break loose from some worldly tie every day. Victory over one sin upon right grounds will pave the way to an easy conquest of all.

I never look upon a corpse without thinking that my soul will one day behold my own. What an awful moment! How happy will be the sight if soul and body have lived together for eternity! how dreadful if they have not! and what a call is there to make sure of rejoicing then!

Christ never comes into the soul unattended; he brings the Holy Spirit with him, and the Spirit his train of gifts and graces. Lay the foundation in him, and leave it to him to raise God's building upon it.

The mystery of the Gospel, as distinguished from the law, consists in changing the order of two words. One says, "Do and live;" the other says, "Live and do."

I cannot love my neighbor as myself till I love God with all my heart. I cannot love God but from a sense of his love to me in the forgiveness of my sins, and I cannot receive forgiveness from him as a benefit till I know my want of it.

If I was to live to the world's end, and do all

the good that man can do, I must still cry, "Mercy!" Why, then, should I be unwilling or afraid to die this moment, with a sense of God's pardoning love, when I can have no other claims to salvation if I was to live forever?

One would think it tolerably modest to say that God knows the way to heaven better than we do, and that it is lawful for him to prescribe to us the terms of our admission into it; and yet there is no proposition more generally ridiculed.

God pardons in order to cleanse. Whoever expects forgiveness without any thought or desire of being cleansed, cannot receive it. It is impossible for God to forgive an unrepenting sinner; and he does not repent who does not purpose and wish to be changed.

If I have faith in Christ, I shall love him; if I love him, I shall keep his commandments; if I do not keep his commandments, I do not love him; if I do not love him, I do not believe in him.

Repent, and believe; believe, and love; love, and obey; obey in love, and be as happy as you can be in this world.

The spirit in the children of God is like an organ; one man is one stop; another, another; the sound is different, the instrument the same, but music in all.

FROM FENELON.

We must never be astonished at temptations, be they never so outrageous. On this earth all is temptation. Crosses tempt us by irritating our pride, and prosperity by flattering it. Our life is a continual combat, but one in which Jesus Christ fights for us. We must pass on unmoved while temptations rage around us, as the traveler, overtaken by a storm, simply wraps his cloak more closely about him, and pushes on more vigorously toward his destined home.

Be never troubled at the loss of the sensible presence of God; but, above all, beware of seeking to retain him by a multitude of argumentative and reflective acts. Be satisfied during the day, and while about the details of your daily duties, with a general and interior view of God, so that if asked at any moment whither your heart is tending, you may answer with truth that it is toward God, though the attention of your mind may then be engrossed by something else. Be not troubled by the wanderings of your imagination which you cannot restrain; how often do we wander through the fear of wandering, and the regret that we have done so! What would you say of a traveler who, instead of constantly advancing in his journey, should employ his time in anticipating the falls which he might suffer, or in weeping over the place where one had happened? On, on, you would say to him; on, without looking behind or stopping.

We must proceed, as the apostle bids us, that we may abound more and more. The abundance of the love of God will be of more service in correcting us than all our restlessness and selfish reflections.

FROM MADAM GUYON.

There is time for every thing in our lives; but the maxim that governs every moment is, that there should be none useless; that they should all enter into the order and sequence of salvation; that they are all accompanied by duties which God has allotted with his own hand, and of which he will demand an account; for from the first instance of our existence to the last, he has never assigned us a barren moment, nor one which we can consider as given up to our own discretion. The great thing is to recognize his will in relation to them.

When the soul is once turned toward God, it finds a wonderful facility in continuing steadfast in conversion; and the longer it remains thus converted, the nearer it approaches and the more firmly it adheres to God; and the nearer it draws to him, it is of necessity the further removed from the creature, which is so contrary to him; so that it is so effectually established in conversion that the state becomes habitual and, as it were, natural.

FROM HANNAH MORE.

The intellectual vices, the spiritual offenses, may destroy the soul without much injuring the credit. These have not, like voluptuousness, their seasons of alternation and repose. Here the principle is in continual operation. Envy has no interval; ambition never cools; pride never sleeps. The principle, at least, is always awake. An intemperate man is sometimes sober, but a proud man is never humble. Where vanity reigns, she reigns always. These interior sins are more difficult of extirpation, they are less easy of detection, more hard to come at, and as the citadel sometimes holds out after the outworks are taken, these sins of the heart are the latest conquered in the moral welfare.

Say not that the requisitions of religion are severe; ask, rather, if they are necessary. If a thing must absolutely be done, if eternal misery will be incurred by not doing it, it is fruitless to inquire whether it be hard or easy. Inquire only whether it be indispensable, whether it be commanded, whether it be practicable. It is a well-known axiom in science that difficulties are of no weight against demonstrations. The duty on which our eternal state depends is not a thing to be debated, but done. The duty which is too imperative to be evaded, too important to be neglected, is not to be argued about, but performed. To sin on quietly because you do not intend to sin always, is to live on a reversion which will probably never be yours.

The politician, the warrior, and the orator find it peculiarly hard to renounce in themselves that wisdom and strength to which they believe the rest of the world are looking up. The man of station or of genius, when invited to the self-denying duties of Christianity, as well as he who has "great possessions," goes away sorrowing.

But to know that they must end stamps vanity on all the glories of life; to know that they must end soon stamps infatuation not only on him who sacrifices his conscience for their acquisition, but on him who, though upright in the discharge of his public duties, discharges them without any reference to God. Would the conqueror or the orator reflect when the laurel crown is placed on his brow, how soon it will be followed by the cypress wreath, it would lower the delirium of ambition, it would cool the intoxication of prosperity.

FROM DYER.

Be upright Christians.

Fear not the fear of men.

Live in love, and live in truth.

Acquaint yourselves with yourselves.

Learn humility from Christ's humility.

Cleave closest to that truth which is choicest.

Improve that time which will be yours but for a time.

Do good in the world with the goods of the world.

Be willing to want what God is not willing to give.

Take nothing upon trust, but all upon trial.

Take those reproofs best which you need most.

Crucify your sins that have crucified your Saviour.

Labor more for inward purity than for outward felicity.

Let it be thy art in duty to give God thy heart in duty.

Be diligent in the means, but make not an idol of the means.

Set the watch of your lives by the Sun of Righteousness.

Hear the best men, read the best books, keep the best company.

Set out for God at your beginning, and hold out until your ending.

Meditate often on the four last things: death, which is most certain; judgment, which is most strict; hell, which is most doleful; heaven, which is most delightful.

FROM PERE LA COMBE.

Faith and the cross are inseparable: the cross is the shrine of faith, and faith is the light of the cross.

How rare it is to behold a soul in an absolute abandonment of selfish interests, that it may devote itself to the interests of God!

In the commencement of the spiritual life our hardest task is to bear with our neighbor; in its progress, with ourselves, and in its end, with God.

How are we directed in the law to love ourselves? In God, and with the same love that we bear to God; because, as our true selves are in him, our love must be there also.

The more the darkness of self-knowledge deepens about us the more does the divine truth shine in the midst.

God gives us gifts, graces, and natural talents, not for our own use, but that we may render them to him. He takes pleasures in giving and in taking them away, or in so disposing of us that we cannot enjoy them; but their grand use is to be offered in a continual sacrifice to him, and by this he is most glorified.

I have never found any who prayed so well as those who had never been taught how. They who have no master in man have one in the Holy Spirit.

He who has a pure heart will never cease to pray, and he who will be constant in prayer shall know what it is to have a pure heart.

The harmlessness of the dove consists in not judging another, the wisdom of the serpent in distrusting ourselves.

FROM MATTHEW HENRY.

Religion and piety are the best securities of a nation.

We cannot expect too little from man or too much from God.

Piety is the best friend to prosperity.

Those deceive themselves who expect advantage by friendship with those who are enemies to God. It but exposes them to constant temptation, and at length draws them to sin.

Those that admire themselves despise God.

They that drive the good Spirit away from them do, of course, become a prey to the evil one.

When God has given us rest, we must take heed of slothfulness.

Love not sleep, love not sport, love not sauntering; but love business, serving the Lord with diligence.

Come here and see the victories of the cross. Christ's wounds are thy healing, his agonies thy repose, his conflicts thy conquests, his groans thy songs, his pains thine ease, his shame thy glory, his death thy life, his sufferings thy salvation.

FROM RICHARD BAXTER.

A heavenly mind is the nearest and truest way to a life of comfort. The countries far north are cold and frozen because they are distant from the sun. What makes such frozen, uncomfortable Christians, but their living so far from heaven? And what makes others so warm in comforts, but their living higher, and having nearer access to God? When the sun in the spring draws nearer to our part of the earth, how do all things congratulate its approach! The earth looks green, the trees shoot forth, the plants revive, the birds sing, and all things smile upon us. If we would but try this life with God, and keep these hearts above, what a spring of joy would be within us! How should we forget our winter sorrows! How early should we rise to sing the praises of our Creator! O Christians, get above!

The heavenly Christian is the lively Christian. It is our strangeness to heaven that makes us so dull. How will the soldier hazard his life, and the mariner pass through storms and waves, and no difficulty keep them back, when they think of an uncertain perishing treasure! What life then would it put into a Christian's endeavors if he would frequently think of his everlasting treasure! We run so slowly and strive so lazily because we so little mind the prize. Set your affections on things above.

Very shortly thou wilt see thy glass run out, and say to thyself, " My life is done! my time is gone! It is past recalling! There is nothing now but heaven or hell before me!" Where, then, shouldst thy heart be now?

You are often asking, "How shall we know that we are truly sanctified?" Here you have an infallible sign from the mouth of Jesus Christ himself: "Where your treasure is, there will your heart be also." God is the saint's treasure and happiness; heaven is the place where they must fully enjoy him. A heart, therefore, set upon heaven is no more but a heart set upon God, and surely a heart set upon God through Christ is the truest evidence of saving grace. When learning will be no proof of grace; when knowledge, duties, gifts, will fail; when arguments from thy tongue or hand may be confuted; yet then will this, from the bent of thy heart, prove thee sincere.

FROM BISHOP JEAN PIERRE CAMUS.

Be devoted in your calling. Religion adapts itself to any lawful state. Fulfill every duty which your vocation lays upon you rather than seek to cultivate graces to which you are not specially bound. That zeal lacks discretion which would introduce into common life customs which befit only the sick-room or the cloister. Let time, place, individual position, and circumstances be duly weighed. Some people want cherries at Christmas and sleighing in August, not content to take things in their season. Such erratic brains are not easy to reason with.

Love and devotion are as much akin to each other as flame is to fire. Love is a spiritual fire, and when it bursts forth into a flame, we call it devotion; devotion only adds to the fire of love that glowing flame which makes it ready, active, and diligent, not merely in keeping God's commandments, but in obeying his heavenly inspirations and counsels.

I do not agree with those who think it impossible to lead a saintly life in this present evil world. One who has God's grace, and strives to preserve a pure heart, need not fear; there is no position so dangerous but may be held safely under this heavenly protection. We find Abraham among idolaters, Lot amid the grossest sinners, and Job in the land of Uz, always united to God, their purity spotless, their love and humility overflowing.

Some fish improve in flavor when they leave the sea and go up the sweeter inland waters; and so some souls do but redouble their fervent piety when duty calls them into scenes which naturally tend to foster carelessness.

Few people accept what is, nevertheless, a great truth, that a faithful, upright soul is more

closely and intimately united to God amid desolation and loneliness than in sensible devotion
and consolation. If a soul is engrossed by the
consolations God gives, it sometimes loses sight
of the giver: those bees which make most wax
are said to make the least honey.

Blessed is the soul which continues steadfast
amid all the dryness, desolation, and wickedness,
which serve as the crucible wherein the pure gold
of love is refined and purified. Blessed is he who
bears the proving trial patiently. "After He
hath proved me, I shall come forth as gold." The
day will come when I shall serve and praise him.

From Bishop Francis de Sales.

Most of the faults committed by good people
arise from their not maintaining a sufficiently
constant recollection of the presence of God.

O what a blessed thing it is to live in God; to
work for God; to rejoice in God only! Henceforth, by his grace, I will be nothing to any one,
and none shall be aught to me, save in and for
God only. I hope to achieve this through a fervent humiliation of my soul before him.

Spiritual progress depends less upon doing a
great deal than upon the spirit of fervent love
which prompts what is done. One good work

15

fervently performed is more acceptable in God's sight than many done in a languid or slovenly way.

How watchfully we ought to cultivate the little virtues which grow beneath the foot of the cross, inasmuch as they are watered with the very blood of the Son of God. Such are humility, patience, gentleness, kindness, forbearance, calmness, good temper, heartiness, pity, ready forgiveness, simplicity, frankness, and the like. These virtues are like violets growing in a shady nook, fed by the dew of heaven, and, though unseen, shedding forth a sweet and precious odor.

He who loves earnestly longs earnestly; he who longs earnestly will seek earnestly; he who seeks earnestly is sure to find; and he who finds grace finds life and salvation in the Lord. We ought to ask nothing so urgently as a pure, holy love for our Saviour. O how we ought to long after this love, and love this longing!

The truest sign that we love God only in all things is when we love him equally in them all. He is always the same, and the inequalities of our love spring from our earthly attachments to something that is not of him. How prone we are to love the world.

It is impossible to remain long stationary. He who does not win loses ; he who does not rise higher upon the ladder must go down ; he who is not a conqueror must be conquered in this strug-gle. We are surrounded by foes, and unless we fight we must perish. But if we fight we are sure to succeed, and if we succeed we shall win a glorious victory, and receive our crown of triumph.

However far advanced toward perfection, we need perpetual watchfulness, for the passions are prone to rekindle even in those who have for years followed the religious life, and made great progress therein.

He who best knows how to mortify his natural inclinations is most open to supernatural inspira-tions.

The Spirit ought to treat the body as its child, when obedient, and not overwhelm it; but if it revolts, it must be treated as a rebellious subject, even as St. Paul says, "I chastise my body, and keep it under."

Truth which is not charitable springs from a charity which is not true.

In time of spiritual depression we ought to work all the harder to prove our faithfulness. One act done amid dryness of spirit is worth many performed with delight—the love which prompts it is deeper, though less agreeable to one's self.

Do not sow a crop of good intentions in another man's garden, but cultivate your own diligently. Do not wish to be any thing save what you are, but strive to be that perfectly. Fix all your thoughts on that, and on bearing every cross, great and small, which it involves. Believe me, this is the real secret, though so little appreciated, of spiritual direction.

Be at peace, and let your soul feed upon the sweetness of heavenly love, without which our hearts were lifeless, our life joyless. Give no place to sadness, the great enemy of devotion. What should sadden one who serves our everlasting Joy? Nothing save sin ought to vex or grieve us; and even when sorry for sin, holy joy and hope should come to the rescue. When David had poured out all his sorrows, he yet exclaimed, "In God's word will I rejoice; in the Lord's word I will comfort me."

FROM OTHERS.

A religion that never suffices to govern a man will never suffice to save him; that which does not sufficiently distinguish one from a wicked world will never distinguish him from a perishing world.—HOWE.

The aggregate amount of Christian duties may be reduced to three things : faith, obedience, and patience; the vital principle which animates them all, submission. Faith is submission to the oracles of God; obedience is submission to the commanding will of God; patience is submission to the chastisement of God.—SOUTH.

You must hold intercourse with God, or your soul will die; you must walk with God, or Satan will walk with you; you must grow in grace, or you will lose it; and you cannot do this but by appropriating to this object a portion of your time, and diligently employing suitable means.— CECIL.

Carry religion into common life is Caird's sensible suggestion. Make perishable things the seed of immortality. No work done for Christ decays. No action that helps to mold the deathless mind of a saint of God is ever lost. Live for Christ in the world, and you carry out with you into eternity all of the results of the world's business that are worth the keeping.

A soul that is humble, says Durant, will be content to tarry days, weeks, or years for the Lord. If God will not raise him up now he will wait in hope that he may hereafter. Surely it is but reason we should wait with patience till God raise us out of the pits of sadness and dejection, since he waited so long for our rising out of the pits of sinfulness and defilement.

When you lie down at night compose your spirits as if you were not to awake till the heavens be no more. And when you awake in the morning; consider that new day as your last, and live accordingly. Surely that night cometh of which you will never see the morning, or that morning of which you will never see the night; but which of your mornings or nights will be such, you know not.

THE END.

www.ingramcontent.com/pod-product-compliance
Lightning Source LLC
Chambersburg PA
CBHW030316270326
41926CB00010B/1392